HOW TO RUN A ONE MINUTE PRACTICE

A GUIDE FOR PHYSIOTHERAPISTS, CHIROPRACTORS, PODIATRISTS, OSTEOPATHS AND ALLIED HEALTH PROFESSIONALS WANTING TO EARN MORE, WORK LESS AND ENJOY THEIR LIVES

PAUL WRIGHT

HOW TO RUN A ONE MINUTE PRACTICE

Physio Professor Pty Ltd,
PO Box 574, Swansea, NSW, Australia, 2281

ISBN 978-0-9945091-0-9

Cover design: Omini
Internal design and layout: Lankshear Design
Internal illustrations and photos: shutterstock.com

PREFACE

By opening this book, you have already taken the first step in your journey towards owning a thriving health business that delivers you and your family more income, more time and the freedom to do the things you enjoy most.

Congratulations!

This book is the culmination of over 20 years of experience gained from not only running my own health businesses but from working closely with health business owners around the world.

Many of these owners are part of my elite One on One Coaching Program, members of my "Profit Club" health business mentor program, have purchased my "Practice Acceleration Program", "Ultimate Patient Attraction System" or "Ultimate Front Desk Training System". Many have also participated in my live seminars and workshops.

If you implement the steps and systems outlined in this book, you will see an incredible transformation in your health business and in the quality of your life.

Guaranteed.

You would have already noticed this book is not a regular – long copy book – it is what is called a "Mini-Book" – or "Picture Book" – and will take you no longer than 45 minutes to read.

What could be more appropriate for a book titled *How to Run a One Minute Practice* than to make this resource easy to read, quick to implement and full of useful tips and strategies that you can use immediately to help free you from your health business.

I hope you enjoy this mini-book and I look forward to hearing about your business success using the *One Minute Practice* systems.

Paul Wright

BONUS RESOURCES THAT WILL HELP YOU RUN A ONE MINUTE PRACTICE

As space for larger documents and pictures are limited in a book this size – you are able to download a range of **documents, forms and other materials** that will help you run your own *One Minute Practice* by going to:

www.OneMinutePracticeBookBonus.com

At this page you will also be able to register for a **special online learning session** where you can learn more about *How to Run a One Minute Practice*.

INTRODUCTION

- Are you a health business owner frustrated by the amount of time you are required to spend at your practice each and every week?
- Are you disappointed when you miss your child's school events and other important family occasions?
- Are you one of those many practitioners too scared to leave their practice for even a short vacation, worrying about the loss of income and fretting about coming back to so many problems that the holiday just wasn't worth it?

I am pleased to introduce *One Minute Practice*, the health business tracking, systematisation and team measurement system guaranteed to provide you the freedom to run your health business from anywhere in the world in less than one minute a day.

Sound interesting?

Let me tell you the story of how the *One Minute Practice* program was born.

> *"One Minute Practice streamlines all my processes and procedures into one place – once you start using this system it will pay for itself no end."*
> **Justin Blake**, Owner, Podiatry IE, Ireland

I used to be a typical health professional working long hours for inadequate rewards.

Arriving at my clinic early in the morning, I would treat clients all day, struggling to find time to fix staff issues and other business problems. I would finally arrived home in the dark, totally exhausted, to spend a few minutes with the kids (if I was lucky) before trying to catch up on the many practice management issues that I did not have time to complete during the day.

The next morning I would get up early – and do it all over again.

Like so many of you, I was living the nightmare of many well intentioned health professionals. We go to university with dreams of helping people cope better and live more enjoyable (and pain free) lives. Only to discover the real world of health business ownership is a combination of long days, staff dramas, over-reliance on us to do everything – and no time left over for family and friends.

Does this sound familiar?

"I feel like I now have total control of my business again – in one minute I can see exactly what is going on in my business – I would recommend One Minute Practice to any health business owner."
Alex Gazis Morris, Owner, Regional Physiotherapy, Australia

Fortunately I was able to extract myself out of this nightmare before it was too late.

I began by cutting back my consulting hours and spending more time on all those areas of business management I had been neglecting for so many years.

The results were amazing.

I was able to totally systematise my health business, which quickly grew to six different clinics. I stopped treating clients and visited my six clinics for only an hour each week (or fortnight). I didn't even live in the same city as five of them!

Other health business owners soon began asking how I was able to enjoy such a great quality of life whilst running my health businesses remotely.

As a result I started conducting seminars and producing programs where I shared my hard earned business knowledge and experience with fellow health business owners from such specialties as Physiotherapy, Chiropractic, Podiatry, Osteopathy, Massage Therapy – and even including Dentists and Doctors.

This high level of systematisation allowed me to sell my practices, for excellent prices, as I wanted to focus my attention on helping more health business owners regain control of their businesses and their lives.

I also began working with an elite group of health business owners from around the world including Australia, New Zealand, United Kingdom, Canada, Asia and the USA – as part of my One on One Health Business Coaching program – and this is where the idea for *One Minute Practice* originated.

I had been using the key components of the ***One Minute Practice*** system for many years to oversee my health businesses – and these were the exact same components I put into effect for the owners in my private coaching program – with the same stunning impact.

Increased team compliance, greater profits and more freedom for the owner – just like I had in my businesses.

However, as I only work with a limited number of private clients at any one time (and my private program is always sold out – and has a long waiting list) – I was not able to help as many health business owners as I would like.

So it made perfect sense to coordinate these essential components into a cloud based Web Program that can be used by health business owners around the word to oversee their businesses, track their clinic performance, and ensure team compliance with their many protocols and procedures.

These exact components and systems needed to run a *One Minute Practice* will finally be revealed to you in this book.

Let's get started!

"I can now be sure that my admin staff and therapists are following my procedures and systems – I would highly recommend One Minute Practice."

Sean-Michael Latimour, Owner, Sports Enrichment Therapy, Canada

Why do health professionals run poor businesses?

- You have little or no training in business systems in your undergraduate education programs.
- You don't understand the importance of great marketing and sales to the success of your businesses.
- Your teams – all caring health professionals – are not interested in sales and marketing so it is all left up to you – the owner.
- As a health professional you want to help as many people as possible live pain free lives and don't want to be seen as money hungry and only interested in creating business profits.
- You are concerned about your professional reputation and do not want to do anything that will negatively impact that hard earned esteem.
- You think if you provide great technical treatments then word will get out and you will be successful in business.
- You are reluctant to enforce your systems and protocols on your teams for fear of them leaving or of you not being well liked by your staff.

> *"It only takes me ten minutes a day to enter the information for our five Physios and the Occupational Therapists – the forms are really easy – a very simply way to keep a track on everybody – highly recommended."*
> **Pauline Gibson**, Practice Manager, New Zealand

Your lack of business training makes you feel:

- Chained to your business and unable to take time off for fear of the your systems not being followed correctly – assuming you have any systems at all.
- Frustrated that you do everything in the business but are not getting any great reward for your efforts.
- Depressed about how your life has turned out and not enjoying your career anywhere near as much as you thought you would when you started your University training.
- Overwhelmed by the number of things you have to do each and every day – and the list only gets longer.
- Inadequate as a parent or spouse – because you have no time or energy left at the end of each day to spend with your family and friends.
- Like a failure – as you know your business is not worth much if you ever tried to sell it – yet you hear all the time about people selling their businesses for hundreds of thousands of dollars.
- Worried – if anything happened to you, your business would fail and put your family at risk.

"The One Minute Practice Program will give you the peace of mind you need as a health business owner."
Yousuf Syed, Owner, Spine and Sports Physiotherapy, Australia

The Solution

- You must put tried and tested **systems and procedures** in place so you do not need to be physically present in your practice all the time.
- You need to ensure these **systems are followed** by your team and have tracking procedures in place to record that these protocols are being completed.
- There must be **consequences** for team members who fail to follow your systems and protocols.
- You need to understand that the systems and procedures you put in place now will add **thousands of dollars** to the value of your business when you sell it.

"The One Minute Practice has been fantastic – it enables me to put all of my KPI's in one place and I can log in from anywhere and in a moment see exactly how work is doing – all the staff are doing the things I have asked – are the KPI's on track – and that takes me – ONE MINUTE."

Helen Macdonald, Owner of Richmond Physiotherapy, New Zealand

"A business is a commercial profitable enterprise that works without you."

Brad Sugars, Business Expert and Founder of Action Coach International

Hard facts about your *One Minute Practice* journey

- As you start your ***One Minute Practice*** journey you may get pushback and resistance from your current team members – especially from those who are comfortable the way things are currently done in your business and are happy to just get their wages paid into their account each week.
- You may lose some team members who feel uncomfortable by being made to follow systems and being held accountable for their individual performance.
- You MUST treat your practice like a real business – with systems, accountability, measurement and consequences.

"The red and green alerts are ideal for someone like me who is not IT savvy – so I can see exactly what is going on in the business whether I am at the practice or not. One Minute Practice is essential for anyone with a health business."

Paul Rowsen, Owner, Balnarring Physiotherapy, Australia

"I am certainly not one of those who need to be prodded. In fact, if anything, I am the prod." **Winston Churchill**

The Seven Secret System Formula for running a *One Minute Practice*

A *One Minute Practice* is based on **Seven Secret Systems** – which were the cornerstones of my health clinics for over 20 years allowing me to run them remotely – and ultimately – sell them for a great price.

These exact same systems have been used exclusively by members of the *One Minute Practice* online software program and inside the thriving practices of my One on One Private Coaching Clients.

There is no doubt – when you start systematically and methodically implementing these systems into your practice you will notice a profound difference.

You will experience a level of confidence and control – you never believed possible as a health business owner

> *"Very impressed – previously I was overwhelmed by lots of different spreadsheets – whereas with One Minute Practice everything is now in one spot – it is very easy to import my data – extremely useful program – highly recommended."*
> **Russell Mackenzie**, Owner, Adelaide West Physiotherapy and Pilates, Australia

The Seven Secret Systems used to run a *One Minute Practice* are:

1. **New Patient Register**
2. Daily Date Entry
3. Profit and Loss
4. Key Performance Indicators
5. Marketing Planner
6. Checklists
7. Ninety Day Goals

The Seven Secret Systems used to run a *One Minute Practice* can be remembered using the first letter from each of the words below:

"New Daily Protocols Keep Money Coming Non-Stop"

The First System – N is for **New Patient Register**

Secret System One – the New Patient Register (NPR)

Just like key measuring equipment and sensors in a modern jet liner, the New Patient Register feeds key information into the instrument panel of our business. Without this information on our new patients, we are flying blind.

We need to capture important data about each new client in order to assist with their rehabilitation needs (and for effective future marketing initiatives).

We also need to track successful completion of all the steps that each new patient must go through.

The job of the New Patient Register is to capture and display this information and to ensure all new clients complete the necessary steps in their journey – allowing the owner to visually verify that key protocols have been followed and completed.

Here are just some of the key content areas of a great **"New Patient Register" (NPR)**, illustrated with screen snapshots from the *One Minute Practice* software, which is available from **www.OneMinutePractice.com**

Essential components of a New Patient Register (NPR)

Date: the date of the patients initial consultation in your clinic

Patients name: first and last name of the new patient

Therapists name: the name of the therapist who treated the patient on their initial visit

Administration persons name: the front desk team member who explained the new patient welcome information and arranged the clients follow up appointments at the end of the initial visit

Referral source: detailed information about how this client found out about your practice – eg. Dr Smith referral, voucher offer in local newspaper, Google Adwords

Body part: the specific injury area the new clients visit relates to– eg Foot – this is particularly important if you want all clients with a specific injury area to have a certain procedure – eg. all Lower Limb clients to have a computer gait assessment

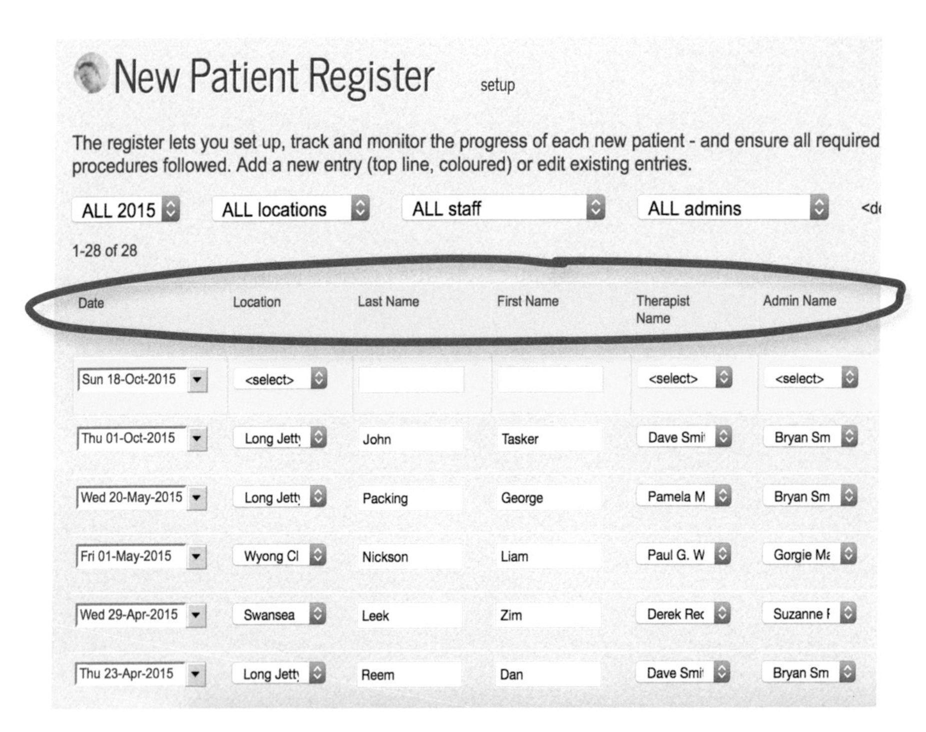
New Patient Register setup

The register lets you set up, track and monitor the progress of each new patient - and ensure all required procedures followed. Add a new entry (top line, coloured) or edit existing entries.

ALL 2015 | ALL locations | ALL staff | ALL admins | <d

1-28 of 28

Date	Location	Last Name	First Name	Therapist Name	Admin Name
Sun 18-Oct-2015	<select>			<select>	<select>
Thu 01-Oct-2015	Long Jett	John	Tasker	Dave Smi	Bryan Sm
Wed 20-May-2015	Long Jett	Packing	George	Pamela M	Bryan Sm
Fri 01-May-2015	Wyong Cl	Nickson	Liam	Paul G. W	Gorgie Ma
Wed 29-Apr-2015	Swansea	Leek	Zim	Derek Rec	Suzanne F
Thu 23-Apr-2015	Long Jett	Reem	Dan	Dave Smi	Bryan Sm

Some essential components of a New Patient Register, screenshot taken from www.OneMinutePractice.com

"One Minute Practice has saved me thousands of dollars in terms of time investment – for a multi-location business like mine, you would easily be saving 5K to 10K a week in revenue just by using this program." **Aaron Hardaker**, Owner, Mid North Coast Physiotherapy, Australia

New patient folder given – YES/NO

All new clients of a *One Minute Practice* **MUST** receive a welcome pack which includes your latest clinic newsletter, general information about your practice, vouchers for a free assessment the new client can give to their family and friends, and details of the other health services you provide.

If you want all new clients to receive a "New Patient Folder" – it is essential that the administration team mark this section as "**YES**" in your NPR.

The key to running a *One Minute Practice* is to be able to quickly scan the NPR and see if there are any "NO's" when it should have been a "YES" – then immediately make the person responsible for this step aware of the oversight.

You can download samples of the contents of a great **New Patient Folder** at:

www.OneMinutePracticeBookBonus.com

"Reduce the time between a step or protocol not being followed, you finding out about it and your team knowing you found out about it."

Paul Wright

A *One Minute Practice* fundamental

New Patient Agreement given and signed – YES/NO

All new clients of a *One Minute Practice* must be made aware of and sign a New Patient Agreement – which is essentially the terms and conditions of doing business with you.

Some essential components of a New Patient Agreement include:

- **Cancellation Policy:** a minimum of 24 hours notice MUST be given or a cancellation fee will be charged
- **Doctor Confirmation:** you have the clients permission to contact their doctor regarding this patients care and treatment progress
- **Referral Policy:** you expect all clients to refer their family and friends to you
- **Re-Booking Procedure:** you expect all clients to book multiple sessions – in advance – at the end of the initial consult (more on this later)
- **Patient Feedback System:** new clients are expected to complete a new patient survey at the end of their initial consultation where they rate the service you and your team deliver
- **Payment Policy:** consultation fees must be made at the time of the consultation (for cash based clients)

All new clients **MUST** read, sign and return the completed **"New Patient Agreement"** to your administration team **before** they begin their initial consultation – even better is for your admin team to sit next to the new client in the reception area and explain each part of the agreement as they complete the form.

You can download an example of a **New Client Agreement** at:

www.OneMinutePracticeBookBonus.com

Recommended Action Plan (RAP) given– YES/NO

The Recommended Action Plan (RAP) or Report of Findings (ROF) is one of the fundamental components of a *One Minute Practice*.

The Action Plan protocol dictates that all new patients are given a written outline or summary which explains the initial plan for this clients future treatments at your practice.

The power of the RAP cannot be ignored and we **highly recommend** that you place this step in your *One Minute Practice* **immediately**.

You can download a sample **Recommended Action Plan** at:

www.OneMinutePracticeBookBonus.com

The true power of the Recommended Action Plan (RAP)

In most Physiotherapy, Chiropractic, Podiatry and Osteopathy businesses the clinic owner is never truly certain how well the other therapists are doing with their rebooking of new clients.

Some therapists schedule one follow up session at a time – others schedule a few sessions in advance – and some simply say "Call me when you can make it back in to see me".

This random booking system leads to **poor client outcomes, low consult numbers and uncertainty** on the part of the patient as to how many treatment sessions they actually require to get a great result.

We recommend all *One Minute Practices* deliver a RAP to all new patients – where you or your therapy team write down exactly how many follow up sessions this client needs in the initial stage of their treatment program.

Eg: Three sessions a week for the next 2 weeks, or once a week for the next 4 weeks.

The patient now knows **exactly what is expected**, your administration team know how many sessions to schedule for this patient and the owner knows how effective each of your team members are at gaining the patients trust and filling their appointment book.

A *One Minute Practice* owner MUST be certain that:

- **100%** of all new patients receive a written action plan – no exceptions.
- Your therapists are all **well trained** in the effective delivery of the plan to the patient – so the therapist is confident in what they say and how they say it.
- Your administration team **schedule all** (or as many as possible) of the consultation outlined on the plan at the end of the initial consultation – this gives the patient the best chance of a successful recovery and also allows the patient to schedule the appointment times most suitable for them.
- Your administration team enters **both** the "Consults Recommended on Action Plan" and the "Actual Number of Follow Up Consultations Booked" into the New Patient Register.
- Your therapy team understand that the initial treatment recommendation is their **best estimate** of the likely treatment number required BUT can be modified – by adding or removing treatment sessions for that patient – during follow up visits.

"The only new patient **NOT** given a written action plan at the end of their first consultation, is the patient who has sadly collapsed and died during this session."

Paul Wright

A *One Minute Practice* fundamental

Consults on Recommended Action Plan (RAP) – a number

On a well drafted and completed action plan – there will be a numerical figure equal to the total number of appointments the therapist has recommended for this patient during the initial stage of care.

For Example: 3 sessions a week for 2 weeks = 6 sessions

1 session a week for 4 weeks = 4 sessions

This total number of **"Consults on RAP"** is then entered in the New Patient Register for that patient.

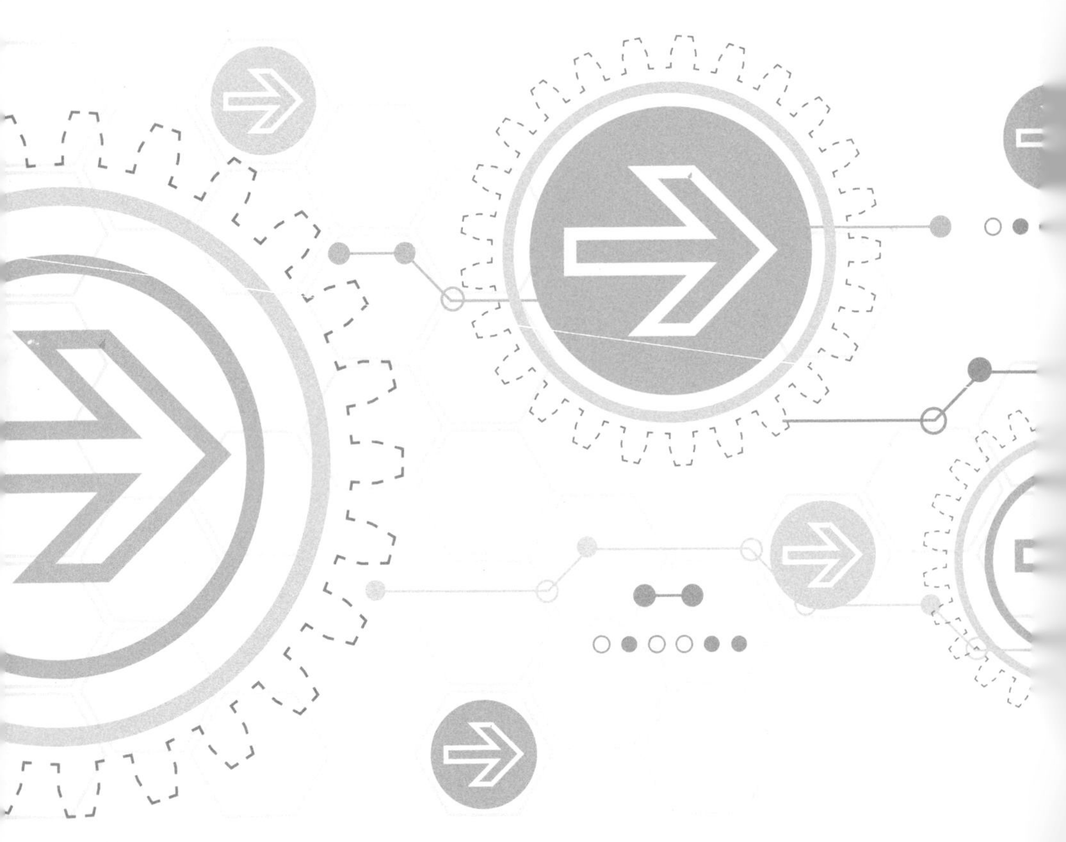

More components of a New Patient Register (NPR)

Future Bookings Made – a Number

"Future Bookings Made" is the actual number of consultations the new patient schedules when they present the written treatment plan to the administration team at the front counter at the end of the initial assessment.

Ideally – the number of "Future Bookings Made" should be as close as possible to the number of treatment sessions the therapist actually recommended on the written RAP.

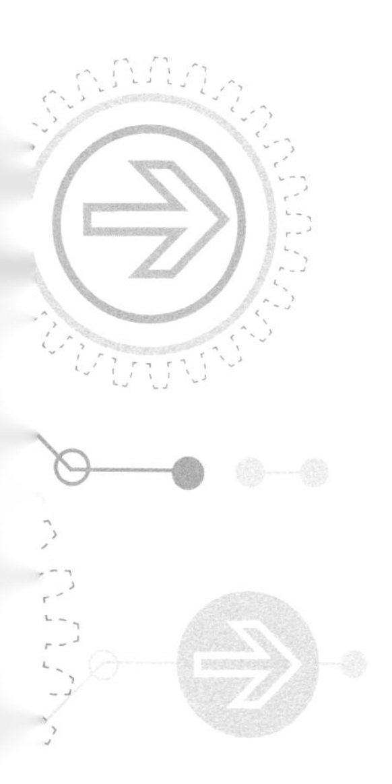

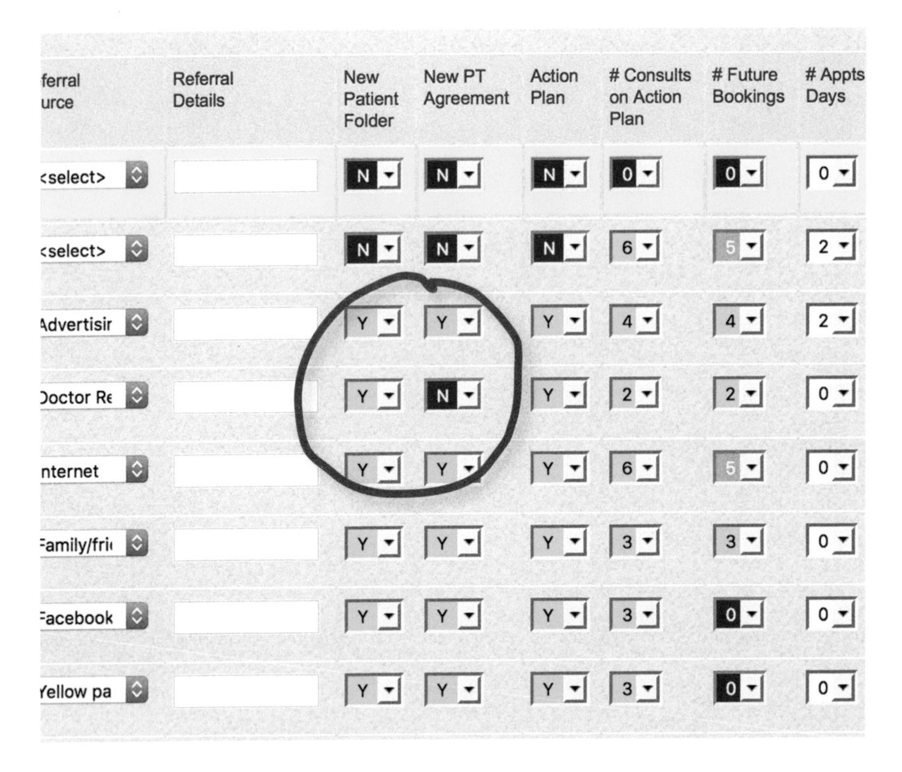

ferral urce	Referral Details	New Patient Folder	New PT Agreement	Action Plan	# Consults on Action Plan	# Future Bookings	# Appts Days
<select>		N	N	N	0	0	0
<select>		N	N	N	6	5	2
Advertisir		Y	Y	Y	4	4	2
Doctor Re		Y	N	Y	2	2	0
nternet		Y	Y	Y	6	5	0
Family/fri		Y	Y	Y	3	3	0
Facebook		Y	Y	Y	3	0	0
Yellow pa		Y	Y	Y	3	0	0

A New Patient Register with Action Plan Given (Y/N), consults on Action Plan, Number of Future Bookings from www.OneMinutePractice.com

Colour coding clearly points out when a system has not been completed, performed incorrectly or not to a suitable standard.

More components of a New Patient Register (NPR)

Number of Appointments in Next 30 Days – a Number

In the majority of acute care allied health clinics – a large percentage of the consultations that are recommended on the initial RAP will be scheduled and completed in the thirty days immediately following the initial consultation.

It is essential for *One Minute Practice* owners to know how many actual treatment sessions each new patient physically attended in this thirty day period – not including the initial session.

Obviously – the "Number of Appointments in Next 30 Days" data **cannot be added** to the NPR until thirty days after the initial consultation date – at which time your administration team goes back to the NPR – finds patients that had an initial consult thirty days prior– and enters how many sessions this patients actually attended in this thirty day time period.

Referral Details	New Patient Folder	New PT Agreement	Action Plan	# Consults on Action Plan	# Future Bookings	# Appts 30 Days	Action Comment
	N	N	N	0	0	0	
	N	N	N	6	5	2	
	Y	Y	Y	4	4	2	
	Y	N	Y	2	2	0	
	Y	Y	Y	6	5	0	
	Y	Y	Y	3	3	0	
	Y	Y	Y	3	0	0	
	Y	Y	Y	3	0	0	

One Minute Practice owners become very skilled at comparing the Consults on Action Plan, Number of Future Bookings and Appointments in Next 30 Days columns. An example of a New Patient Register from inside www.OneMinutePractice.com

Note: Obviously the "Number of Appointments in Next 30 Days" data cannot be added until at least 30 days after the date of the initial consultation for this patient, however this gives the owner valuable information regarding the success or failure of the proposed treatment program for this client.

This is GOLD for the *One Minute Practice* owner

You now have a method to track how many follow up consultations your team are recommending, how many treatment sessions are actually booked at the end of the initial assessment – and finally how many sessions this patient completed in the following thirty days – with these key numbers **appearing side by side** in the NPR –colour coded for easy identification.

This is **GOLD** for a health business owner as you are now **ABSOLUTE CERTAINTY** of the performance of your therapists and administration team members – and you **DO NOT** need to be physically at your practice to oversee this protocol.

Consults on Plan	Consults Booked	Consults in 30 Days	
8	8	8	= an ideal outcome – a good trend
6	4	8	= still a solid result

Scheduling trends that concern a *One Minute Practice* owner

As you become more skilled in the analysis of your New Patient Register there are a number of trends that you must discover and act on quickly – here are some of the most common issues this analysis reveals:

Consults on Action Plan	Future Consults	Consults Completed in Next 30 Days
8	8	0

This looked good initially as the therapist recommended 8 follow up sessions and all 8 sessions were booked, however the patient did not attend any of the follow up treatment sessions – you may want to check the therapist gained the patients trust and the patient was happy with the initial assessment and treatment program outlined.

Consults on Action Plan	Future Consults	Consults Completed in Next 30 Days
6	1	1

In this example the therapist seemed to do well with their recommendations but the admin team may have let the therapist down by not making the follow up bookings – then the patient did not complete the treatment program anyway as they only attended one of the suggested 6 follow up appointments.

Consults on Action Plan	Future Consults	Consults Completed in Next 30 Days
2	1	0

In this example the patient may have only required two treatment sessions for their specific problem – however if your other therapists are typically recommending 6-8 sessions for the average new patient and this particular therapist is only recommending 1-2 on the RAP forms – then you may have a problem with this therapist under treating.

One Minute Practices NEVER over-service

The Action Plan protocol and re-booking system suggested in the *One Minute Practice* program is never used to increase profits by over-servicing clients.

In the vast majority of allied health clinics there is actually gross **UNDER-SERVICING** where sloppy patient explanations and ineffective re-booking systems cause poor outcomes for the client – simply because the patient **DID NOT** receive enough treatment sessions to correct their problem.

It is no surprise the most experienced therapists – and the ones that get the **best outcomes** for their patients – are the therapists who typically see the client for the most sessions, back their ability to make a difference, and deliver clear and definite re-booking instructions to their clients.

You are the expert

For owners, administration team members and therapists who have ever said or heard a patient in your practice asked this question – which we call **"the question of death"** in private practice:

"Are you re-booking?"

Shame on you!!!!

Since when does the patient determine when they need to make their next appointment?

You are the university trained professional who honed your skills for many years so you can be in the position to prescribe the treatment schedule for your clients that will deliver them the best possible outcome.

The re-booking frequency **IS NOT** the patients decision – it is YOURS and yours ALONE.

More Components of a New Patient Register (NPR)

Here are some other steps and protocols you may want to include in your NPR – however – make sure the fundamental procedures of "Recommended Action Plan", "Number of Future Bookings Made", and "Consults Completed in Next Thirty Days" are being done 100% of the time – before adding new steps like the ones below:

Follow up call done – Yes/No

In a *One Minute Practice* – all new clients should receive a courtesy phone call within the first 24 hours following the initial consult.

Something like:

"Hi Mary, it's Paul from XYZ Health Care – just checking that all is OK following our session earlier today and that you understood the treatment plan I described in the session. Do you have any questions you forgot to ask in the session today?"

This call ideally ends with the follow up appointment reminder ie: *"That's great – I will see you at 3pm tomorrow – where I will show you the second exercise in the recovery plan that will get you ready for that marathon in 3 weeks – see you then".*

If you want the "Follow Up Call Made" step to be completed for each new patient – simply add a column in your NPR then watch for any "NO's" on the NPR for this column– and raise the issue immediately if you notice this step has not been completed.

"Select a relatively small number of essential steps and procedures (say 3-6) – and ensure these steps are being completed on your New Patient Register – **before** adding new and more complex protocols."

Paul Wright

A *One Minute Practice* fundamental

Feedback score – admin/ therapists/overall clinic

In a *One Minute Practice* – all new clients are asked to complete a written feedback from at the end of their initial consultation.

Our favourite feedback from is where the new client answers this question on a written form given to them at the end of the initial assessment session:

"On a 0 to 10 scale – how likely is it that you will recommend our clinic to your family and friends – with 10 being Highly Likely and a Zero being Highly Unlikely".

The best feedback forms have a separate score for the admin teams performance, the therapists performance and for the overall clinic performance.

These three feedback scores are then recorded on the NPR under the headings "Feedback Score Admin", "Feedback Score Therapist", and "Feedback Score Overall Clinic".

The feedback score system a great way to check that your team are satisfying the needs of the client – and allowing you to run the practice remotely.

You can download a sample Feedback Form at:

www.OneMinutePracticeBookBonus.com

Email address added to e-database – Yes/No

In a *One Minute Practice* – all new clients are asked for their email address and for permission to send them updates and extra clinic resources following the initial visit.

Many clinics then enter the new clients email address into an external email delivery program (or their Practice Management System if email marketing compliant) – where a "Welcome to the Practice" email is immediately sent and you use a well structured follow up email marketing program to help the client stay fit, healthy and part of your business family.

You can download a sample "New Patient Welcome Email" at:

www.OneMinutePracticeBookBonus.com

New patient welcome letter sent – Yes/No

In a *One Minute Practice* all new clients are posted a "Welcome to the Practice" direct mail letter that includes information similar to the "New Patient Agreement".

The "Welcome to the Practice" letter is a great opportunity to remind the new client of the terms and conditions of doing business with you and also allows you a chance to give the new patient added bonuses or resources.

With email opening rates on the decline – you need to use many different media methods to stay in touch with your database and prevent them from moving to your competitors.

You can download an example of a sample new patient welcome letter at:

www.OneMinutePracticeBookBonus.com

Computer foot assessment or specific protocol completed – Yes/No

In a *One Minute Practice*, depending on your exact speciality, there may be a number of specific tests or procedures that you want all new clients to be taken through as they begin their new client journey.

In some clinics this may be a computer foot assessment – it may be a "Chronic Pain Survey" or your "Spinal Screening Protocol".

Regardless of the exact step you want done – you need to set it up in your NPR so your team have to record that this procedure was actually completed.

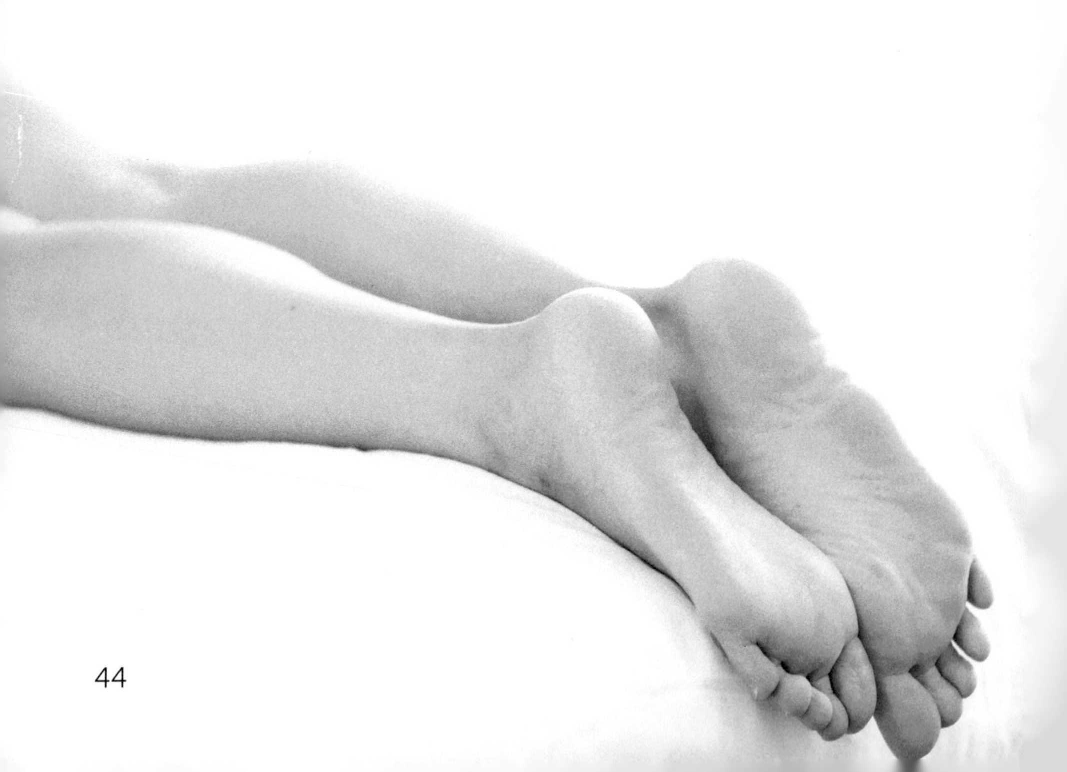

# Future Bookings	# Appts 30 Days	Follow Up Call Done	Feedback Form Done	Score Admin	Score Therapist	Score Clinic	Emailed, added to E-database	Welcome Letter Sent
0	0	N	N	0	0	0	N	N
5	2	N	N	0	0	0	N	N
4	2	Y	Y	0	0	9	Y	Y
2	0	Y	Y	0	6	10	Y	Y
5	0	Y	Y	8	7	6	Y	Y
3	0	Y	Y	0	10	10	Y	Y
0	0	Y	Y	0	10	3	Y	Y
0	0	Y	Y	0	10	10	Y	Y

More options for a New Patient Register from inside www.OneMinutePractice.com

"Remove discretion at the operating level of the business."

Michael Gerber, Author of *The E-Myth Revisited*

Final words on your New Patient Register (NPR)

A well constructed and monitored NPR is like the "**Policeman of Your Business**" – as it has the ability to let you know quickly and easily if your systems are being followed and all team members are on track.

It is also an easily customisable tool, however, where you can add and remove steps at any time.

When you first launch your NPR – watch it closely – and jump up and down the moment a step is missed.

If your team know you are watching the NPR closely – and acting quickly when steps are missed – the power of your NPR will dramatically increase the level of control you have in your health business and greatly increase your profits.

Secret System Two – Daily Data Entry

1. New Patient Register
2. **Daily Date Entry**
3. Profit and Loss
4. Key Performance Indicators
5. Marketing Planner
6. Checklists
7. Ninety Day Goals

The Seven Secret Systems used to run a *One Minute Practice* can be remembered using the first letter from each of the words below:

"New Daily Protocols Keep Money Coming Non-Stop"

The Second Secret System – D is for Daily Date Entry

Secret System Two – Daily Data Entry (DDE)

Let me get one thing straight – I am a huge fan of Practice Management Software (PMS) systems and believe all great clinics **MUST** have a comprehensive PMS system to be truly successful.

However – there is a range of important business data that is either not collected by your PMS – is incorrectly calculated – or is deemed unimportant by your therapists or administration team members.

This is why all *One Minute Practice* owners need a system to collect a range of data each and every day – which enables them to track very closely their clinics and team members performance.

Like the NPR, the Daily Data Entry feeds key information into the instrument panel of our business.

Without the Daily Data Entry, we the business owners are again flying blind.

The fact this data is entered daily – preferably by the administration team – saves you time and reduces the stress of getting the key numbers at the end of the month – a task many owner rarely get to or is not done at all.

The information entered into your Daily Data Entry system should relate to a specific Key Performance Indicator (KPI) that you use to track your team or business performance.

Some key points about the Daily Data Entry (DDE) system

If your PMS is able to give you a simple report with accurate data then print this report and **copy the information** into your DDE system – do not re-invent the wheel.

Get your admin team to complete the DDE systems **first thing in the morning** so the data collection is systematic and relates to the previous days activity.

If you are closed on weekends then the data for Friday is entered on **Monday** morning.

It should not take your administration team more than **a few minutes** per therapist to enter the previous days key data.

A *One Minute Practice* warning

Your administration team (and even your PMS support staff) will question **why you are entering some of this data** into a Daily Data Entry system – when it may already appear in a PMS report.

The answer is that this data feeds into a number of key business performance measures within *One Minute Practice* that are critical to your practice and cannot be found inside the PMS.

You will also find that the simple fact that you are extracting some key numbers from your PMS, moving this data to a new system, and then using this information to complete team member reviews and monitor Key Performance Indicators – is enough to **raise awareness of this data and improve team performance**.

Essential components of the Daily Data Entry (DDE) system

Date – the date this information refers to.

Therapists or Admin Team Members Name – the team member for which the data relates.

Admin Hours Worked – the number of hours this admin team member worked and expects to be paid for on this day.

Therapist Hours Worked – the total number of hours the therapist was in this clinic on this day – including meetings, training etc – but excluding lunch and unpaid breaks – ie. how many hours was the therapist in the clinic and expecting to be paid for?

Consulting Hours – the number of hours the therapist was available to be booked with clients this day.

Patient Hours – the number of hours the therapist spent actually treating patients this day – ie. only count actual face to face contact hours for this therapist with clients – do not count meeting, training, lunch, cancellations or DNA hours where the spots were not filled.

Utilisation rate

Patient Hours as a % of Consulting Hours is termed "**Utilisation Rate**" and is effectively telling you how fully booked (or Utilised) a therapist is each day, week, month or year.

From experience this data is most accurately taken from a visual observation and analysis of the previous days appointment diary and not from your PMS.

One Minute Practice Staffing Tip

Once your therapy team have reached a **Utilisation Rate of Above 75%** – you need to be looking for more team members to further increase your profits, reduce your own consulting hours (if you are still treating clients) and reduce the impact should a current team member leave your business.

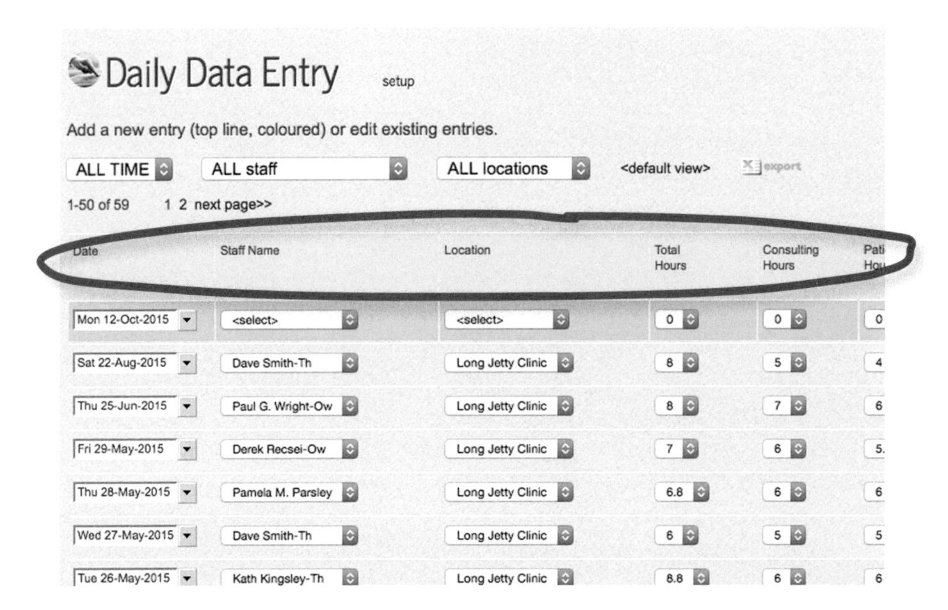

Possible components of a Daily Data Entry system from www.OneMinutePractice.com

More possible components of the Daily Data Entry (DDE) spreadsheet

Number of New Patients – the number of new patients seen by this therapist on this day.

Number of Stock Items Sold – the number of a particular stock items sold by this therapist on this day.

Note – the DDE section is made up of the key numbers you want to record and use to measure, train and manage your team.

Patient Hours	Admin Hours	Number of DNA Appointments	Number of Cancelled Appointments	Wasted Therapist Hours	Consult Billings ($)	Stock/Oth Billings ($)
0:00	0:00	0	0	0:00		
1:00	0	0	0	0:00	70	
7:00	0	0	0	0:00	100	120
0:00	0	0	0	0:00		
2:50	0	0	0	0:00		
0	2:00	0	0	0:00		
5:30	0	0	0	0:00		970
1:30	0	0	0	0:00		
2:00	0	0	0	0:00		
1:30	0	0	0	0:00		
4:00	0	0	0	0:00		

More components of the Daily Data Entry, from www.OneMinutePractice.com

Final words on your Daily Data Entry (DDE)

The information collected from the **New Patient Register** and the **Daily Data Entry** systems will be used in the upcoming **Key Performance Indicators** (KPI) and **Profit and Loss** (P&L) sections of the *One Minute Practice* program which will allow you to oversee and measure the performance of your team from anywhere in the world.

Important – when you first launch your DDE – watch it closely – and jump up and down the moment the previous days data is not collected and entered.

If your team realise you are failing to keep a close eye on the Daily Data Entry protocol – this system will fade away like most of your previous steps and protocols.

Do not let this happen to your *One Minute Practice*.

The Daily Date Entry automatically feeds information into one of the primary instruments in the cockpit of your business, namely the Profit and Loss Analysis.

Let us now examine this critical element of your *One Minute Practice*.

Secret System Three – Profit and Loss

1. New Patient Register
2. Daily Date Entry
3. **Profit and Loss**
4. Key Performance Indicators
5. Marketing Planner
6. Checklists
7. Ninety Day Goals

The Seven Secret Systems used to run a *One Minute Practice* can be remembered using the first letter from each of the words below:

"New Daily Protocols Keep Money Coming Non-Stop"

The Third Secret System – P is for **Profit and Loss**

Secret System Three – Profit and Loss (P&L)

From years of dealing with health business owners around the world – very few have been able to tell me on a month by month basis – **the profitability of their businesses**.

Most owners have no idea if they are paying excessive rent, are overpaying for administration support, or paying their therapy staff so much that there is no profit left for them at the end of the month.

What the majority of health business owners do – is look at their appointment diary – and if there are lots of consultations and very few empty slots – think things are fine.

The slightly sharper ones send their shoebox of receipts to their accountant once a year and wait with baited breath for the accountant to tell them if they are profitable or not.

Others simply look at their bank accounts each week (sometimes each day) and hope like hell there is enough money to pay next weeks wages.

The most successful business owners – in all areas – not just health care – are the ones who know their critical numbers the best.

The Profit and Loss is one of the primary instruments in the cockpit of your business, something to keep a very close eye on.

What should you include in a *One Minute Practice* Profit and Loss analysis?

Firstly add your monthly practice income including:

- **Consult billing** – not cash takings – but billings – taken from the "Consult Billings" section of the Daily Data Entry or Practice Management Software System. You don't need to manually enter this data into your P&L if you are using the *One Minute Practice* software, since these numbers are automatically fed into your P&L from the "Consult Billings" section of the Daily Data Entry.
- **Stock billing** – not cash takings but billings – taken from the "Stock /Other Billing" in the Daily Data Entry or Practice Management Software System. You don't need to enter this data into your P&L if you are using the *One Minute Practice* software, since these numbers are automatically fed into your P&L from the "Stock /Other Billing" section of the Daily Data Entry
- Other Income – eg. pool rental fees, room rental, other payments.

€'s	January	February	March	April	May
INCOME: edit categories					
Consult Billings	100.00	340.00	652.00	1,400.00	3,891.00
Stock/Other Billings	150.00	100.00	781.00	550.00	1,460.00
Pool Rental	42.00	220.00	140.00	120.00	130.00
Affiliate Income				110.00	
Pilates					
Total Gross Income	**292.00**	**660.00**	**1,573.00**	**2,180.00**	**5,481.00**
WAGE EXPENSES: edit hours					
Admin Wages (incl extra's)		69.60	27.84	71.36	77.47
Therapist Wages (incl extra's)	556.80	78.00	1,123.46	190.08	1,378.05
Owner Consulting (incl extra's)				363.00	392.00
Total Wage Expenses	**556.80**	**147.60**	**1,151.30**	**624.44**	**1,847.52**

Components of P&L from www.OneMinutePractice.com

Then add your monthly expenses:

- **Administration Team Wage** – calendar monthly wage you pay to your administration / front office team – including any extra costs such as Superannuation and Workers Compensation insurance. If you are using the *One Minute Practice* software, these numbers are automatically fed into your P&L via the Daily Data Entry.
- **Therapist Wage** – calendar monthly wage you pay to your therapists team – including any extra costs such as Superannuation and Workers Compensation insurance. If you are using the *One Minute Practice* software, these numbers are automatically fed into your P&L.
- **Owner Consulting Wage** – calendar monthly wage you (the owner) are worth as a consulting therapist – we suggest you use an hourly figure equal to the approximate dollar amount you would need to pay to replace you as a consulting therapist. If you are using the *One Minute Practice* software, these numbers are automatically fed into your P&L.
- **Rent** – the rental you pay each calendar month for your practice.
- **Other Clinic Costs** – all other expenses you must pay to operate your clinic each month – including supplies, laundry, bank fees, insurances, telephone, internet, uniforms, stationary, advertising etc.

OTHER EXPENSES:	edit categories			
Accounting Costs - mthly av.	=100+25	20/5	=13*3	23
Advertising	220	220	220	220
Australia Post	128	236	410	120
Bookkeeping	50	50	50	50
Cleaning	200	200	200	200
Electricity	330	330	330	330
Hicaps fee	39	39	39	39
Insurances	90	90	90	90
Laundry	200	120	165	190

Possible other monthly expenses from www.OneMinutePractice.com

The end result

As a *One Minute Practice* owner you now have at your fingertips a calendar month profit and loss you can use to manage your health business and compare to other months and other years.

However, it is all well and good to now have monthly P&L data that you can use to track the progress of your business – but how do you get the most out of this data and how can it help you run your practice?

A good P&L analysis must include a detailed analysis or **results component** that allows you to ensure that the key income and expenses categories of your business are within suitable ranges.

From our experience the business analysis is best done using a "**Percentage of Gross Income**" system – and it is here that the data starts to make more sense and help you run your business effectively and profitably.

Here are some ***One Minute Practice*** **recommendations** for your health business Profit and Loss analysis. By the way, the underlying metrics are automatically calculated for you if you are using the *One Minute Practice* software.

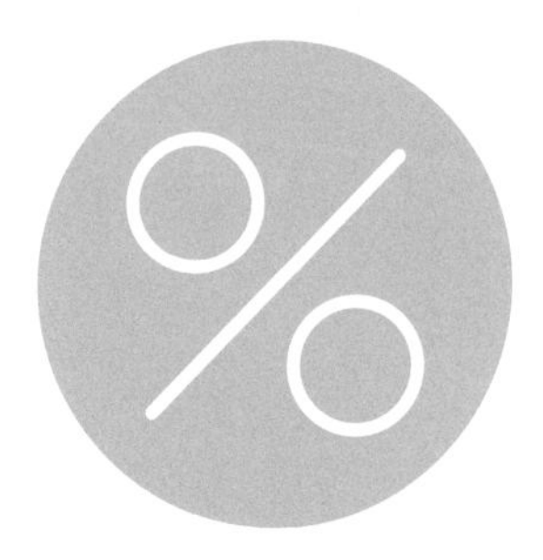

Administration/front office team wage should not exceed 10% of gross billings

When you start doing your P&L *One Minute Practice* style – and notice your total administration wage as a % of gross getting above 10% – you need to look closely at your administration hours and gross billings – and look at ways to control these variables.

- Are your admin team being maximally productive and contributing to the profitability of the business?
- Are you overstaffed in the administration/front office area of your business?
- Have you failed to increase your fees to keep up with administration team wage increases?

Do not let your monthly administration/front office team wages get above 10% of gross monthly billings.

Therapist wage should not exceed 40% of gross billings

The "Therapist Wage as a % of Gross" takes the total therapist wages paid for the calendar month and shows it as a % of gross billing figure.

From our experience we don't like seeing the Therapist Wages as a % of Gross get above 40% – for most small to medium health businesses.

This can be tough in many health businesses when therapists are demanding, and getting, payments of 50% and even 60% of gross – but from our experience these high relative wage expenses make it very difficult to run a profitable health business.

Successful *One Minute Practice*s are able to move their therapy teams onto hourly rates and reduce the therapist wage as a % of gross to **30% and in some cases even 20%**.

This is being achieved by changing the wage structure and increasing billings by offering more exclusive services, a range of high end products and done for you packaged health care solutions to their clients.

Owner Consulting Wage as a % of Gross – this is variable

The "Owner Consulting Wage as a % of Gross" figure can vary depending on how many other therapists are working in the business – and how much consulting the actual owner is actually performing in the practice – so it can be difficult to put a recommended figure here.

However – one of the goals of the *One Minute Practice* program is to free you from the business – and to do this you need to reduce the amount of time you spend treating clients – so you can focus on the more important business development aspects such as marketing, recruitment, program creation and staff development.

Reducing your clinical load will also allow you to focus on even more important areas such as spending time with your family and doing the things you love to do.

So with that goal in mind the most successful *One Minute Practice* owners – actually have a very low "Owner Consulting Wage as a % of Gross" – **with many owners reducing this figure to ZERO** – indicating they now have total freedom – see no clients – can be anywhere at anytime – and yet still have a profitable business.

We will leave the goal for your personal "Owner Consulting Wage as a % of Gross" figure for you to work out – bearing in mind that you may still love treating clients – but the true power of the *One Minute Practice* Profit and Loss system is to show you that you can still have a profitable business even if you are not actively treating clients.

Total wages should be less than 60% of gross billings (50% is better)

The "Total Wage as a % of Gross" figure is the addition of the monthly administration wage, therapist wage and owner consulting wage – so you end up with an overall wage component as part of your *One Minute Practice* Profit and Loss analysis.

This combined wage figure should be less than 60% of gross – however – if you can get it under 50% you are well on your way to running a successful and profitable *One Minute Practice*.

If your "Total Wage as a % of Gross" is much over 50% it becomes increasingly hard for you to remove yourself from the business – as there is just not enough money left over at the end of each month to give you the lifestyle you and your family deserve.

What to do if your total wage as a % of gross is too high

- Increase your consultation fees – always the best place to start in health care businesses.
- Develop a stronger Unique Selling Proposition with specific treatment programs that make price comparison impossible and allow you to increase your fees.
- Renegotiate your teams wage structure so you cover your legal requirements but only pay incentives for excellent performance.
- Become a preferred employer in your area by offering better opportunities and team development so you are not over-reliant on paying top dollar to secure new team members.
- Launch, train and oversee the *One Minute Practice* systems outlined in this book so you can employ less experienced (and cheaper) therapists yet still deliver excellent clinical results.
- Learn how to market your health care business – so you are guaranteed a flood of new and returning clients coming to your practice every day.

Rent should be less than 10% of gross billings

The next figure in your *One Minute Practice* P&L analysis is "Rent as a % of Gross" – which we want to keep under 10% if possible.

You can see how important "Rent as a % of Gross" is to not only the P&L of your existing business – but also the impact it has on your decisions regarding future clinics potential profitability.

You must always keep a close eye on your rent as a % of gross – otherwise you can end up working your tail off and not having any profit to show for it at the end of the month.

Also, do not make the mistake of analyzing future practice locations based solely on the proposed rental amount – or the rental per square metre figure.

I have consistently made the most profit from the clinics where I paid the highest gross rental and the highest rent per square metre.

However – I always made sure there was enough billing potential at these clinics to keep my rent as a % of gross less than 10% – so there was still plenty of profit left in these businesses at the end of each month.

Other clinic costs should be less than 10% of gross billings

The next figure in your *One Minute Practice* Profit and Loss analysis is **"Other Clinic Costs as a % of Gross"** – which is the total of your other clinic expenses – including telephone, advertising, cleaning, bank charges, electricity etc

The *One Minute Practice* goal for your "Other Clinic Costs" is less than 10% of gross.

What to do if your other clinic costs as a % of gross is too high

- Increase your consultation fees – again the best place to start in health care businesses.
- Review your stock ordering procedures and keep a closer eye on inventory – who knows where your clinic supplies are going?
- Review billing procedures to be sure clients are charged for all billable stock items such as strapping tape, exercise tubing, insurer reports and icepacks.
- Look closely at your various monthly expenses and get your administration team to look for cheaper suppliers.

How much profit should your health business generate?

If all goes according to plan you should have something left over – which is your pre-tax profit.

So if our admin is 10% of gross, therapist wage is 40%, owner consulting wage is say 10%, rent is 10% and other clinic costs is 10% – this **should leave you with a 20% pre-tax profit** – as a % of gross amount.

This is the **ABSOLUTE MINIMUM** we would expect for a solidly performing health business – however if you can get your therapy wage under control, boost billings with some smart product sales and price rises – and keep control of your clinic expenses, it is not inconceivable for a pre-tax profit of **30-40% of gross**.

But at least you now know where your money is going – what you need to keep a close eye on – and some idea regarding the value of your business to a potential buyer.

Percentages of Gross Income:					
Admin Wage	8.6%	9.6%	12.3%	9.8%	13.2%
Therapist Wage	41%	29.9%	40.5%	36.5%	39.6%
Owner Consulting Wage	7%	7.1%	2.9%	2.6%	2%
Total Wages Bill	**56.5%**	**46.5%**	**55.7%**	**48.9%**	**54.7%**
Rent/Morgage	6%	7.6%	8.6%	7.1%	8.4%
Other Clinic Costs	11.3%	15.9%	19.1%	16.5%	20%
Profit	**26.2%**	**30%**	**16.7%**	**27.5%**	**16.9%**

An example of a P&L % of Gross Report from www.OneMinutePractice.com

Red numbers indicate areas that are outside expected ratios and must be watched closely.

A comment on the % of gross method used in *One Minute Practice*

The suggestions for your % of gross amounts in the *One Minute Practice* program – have come from our years of experience with small to medium sized health businesses – and have remained true across the majority of health professions.

However – this analysis and recommended percentages may not be as accurate for larger health businesses and those with large stock sale components – think about it – if a large business is grossing $100M a year – I am sure many of you would be happy with a pre-tax profit of 1-2% of $100M.

Where is your money going?

Suggestions for a *One Minute Practice* Profit and Loss Analysis are:

Administration Wage	< 10% of gross
Therapist Wage	< 40% of gross
Owner Consulting	– varies
Total Wage Bill	50-60% of gross
Rent	< 10% of gross
Other Expenses	<10% of gross
Profit	20-30% of gross

As we have seen, the Profit and Loss is a critical top level view of your business. Now we move into the more finely-grained Key Performance Indicators – these KPI's allow you to drill more deeply on areas of potential concern in your business.

Secret System Four – Key Performance Indicators

1. New Patient Register
2. Daily Date Entry
3. Profit and Loss
4. **Key Performance Indicators**
5. Marketing Planner
6. Checklists
7. Ninety Day Goals

The Seven Secret Systems used to run a *One Minute Practice* can be remembered using the first letter from each of the words below:

"New Daily Protocols Keep Money Coming Non-Stop"

The Fourth Secret System –

K is for **Key Performance Indicators**

Secret System Four – Key Performance Indicators (KPI's)

There is no question – one of the most neglected parts of many health businesses – is the measurement of the overall performance of the business and assessment of the performance of team members within that business.

In our years and years of working with health business owners – we have rarely come across any who have accurate, valid and measurable KPI's and goals for their overall clinics – or for their individual team members – and these same owners wonder why the business relies on them so heavily – go figure.

We believe – "**What You Can Measure – You Can Manage**" so it is vital for you to track your teams performance and make them accountable for their overall contribution to the business.

Like the engine monitoring instruments in the cockpit of a modern airliner, anomalies with the KPI's could indicate that your key business drivers may not be providing enough thrust to keep your practice from stalling.

Here are some KPI's we suggest you track and measure in your *One Minute Practice* – noting that these KPI's are automatically calculated and graphed for you if you are using the One Minute Practice software.

Suggested Key Performance Indicators for *One Minute Practice* owners – usually calculated on a monthly basis

Consults Delivered – how many actual consultations that therapist delivered over this time period.

New Patient Number – how many new patients this therapists treated over this time period.

% of New Patients Who Booked Follow Up Appointments – the % of new patients who made at least one follow up booking at the end of their initial consult with that therapist.

Number of New Patients with No Follow Up Booked – the number of new patients who did not make a follow up appointment at the end of the initial consultation with this therapist.

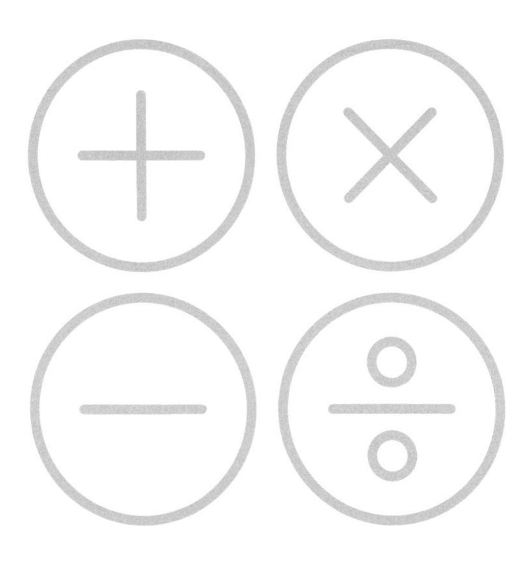

More suggested Key Performance Indicators for *One Minute Practice* owners:

Utilisation Rate – what % of consultation hours for this therapist were spent actually treating patients.

Action Plan Completion % – the percentage new patients who were given an Action Plan by this therapist (should be 100%)

Feedback Score – what was the average patient feedback score for this therapists performance.

Consult Billings $ – the dollar amount for consultation billings by this therapist over this time period

Total Stock Billing $ – the dollar amount of Stock Billings for this therapist over this time period

More suggested Key Performance Indicators for *One Minute Practice* owners:

Billings Per Therapist Hour – the total billings divided by the number of hours worked by this therapist over this time period

Wage as a % of Billings – total wage as a % of the overall billing for this therapist over this time period

Number of Cancellations/No Show – the total number of cancellation or "no show" appointment for this therapists over this time period.

Average Transaction Value – the average payment made by this therapists patients each time they come to the clinic – this is the total therapist billings divided by the number of consults delivered over this time period

More suggested Key Performance Indicators for *One Minute Practice* owners:

Average number of consultation on the new patient action plan – the average number of future appointments this therapist recommends for their new patient on the action plan or future bookings slip – eg if the therapist suggests – 3 times a week for 2 weeks – the number of future consults recommended is 6 – ie 3 x 2 = 6.

Average number of future bookings – the average number of future bookings a new patient actually makes at the end of their first consultation with this specific therapist – the aim is to book all consults the therapist recommends on their action plan – eg. if the therapist recommends 3 treatments a week for 2 weeks – so 6 future bookings – the aim is to book all 6 sessions.

Bookings made % – average number of future appointments made as a percentage of the number of consults recommended for this therapist over this time period.

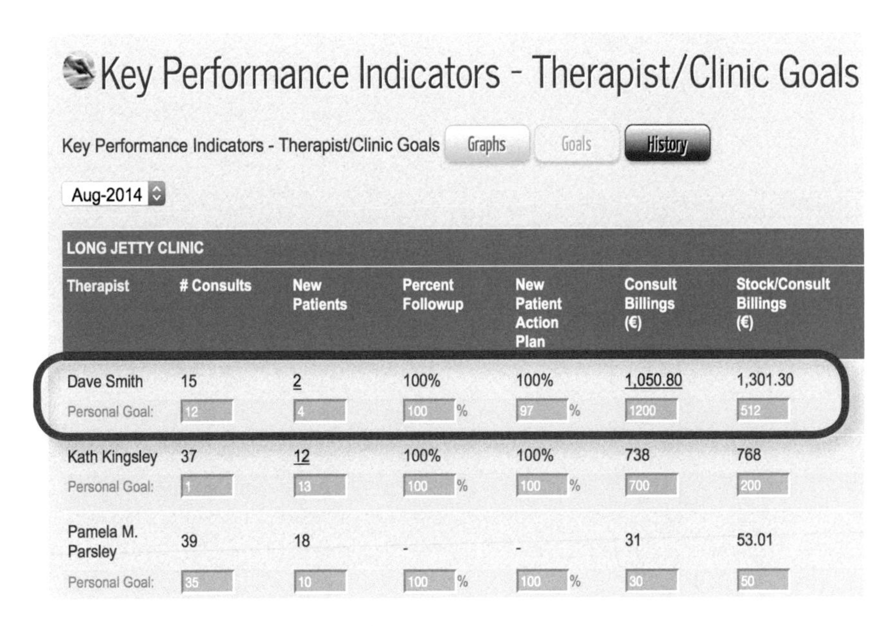

Key Performance Indicators - Therapist/Clinic Goals

Key Performance Indicators - Therapist/Clinic Goals | Graphs | Goals | History

Aug-2014

LONG JETTY CLINIC						
Therapist	# Consults	New Patients	Percent Followup	New Patient Action Plan	Consult Billings (€)	Stock/Consult Billings (€)
Dave Smith	15	2	100%	100%	1,050.80	1,301.30
Personal Goal:	12	4	100 %	97 %	1200	512
Kath Kingsley	37	12	100%	100%	738	768
Personal Goal:	1	13	100 %	100 %	700	200
Pamela M. Parsley	39	18	-	-	31	53.01
Personal Goal:	35	10	100 %	100 %	30	50

You must have goals for each Key Performance Indicator – from inside www.OneMinutePractice.com

Tips on Overseeing Your Team Members KPI's

We suggest you initially monitor just **3-5 KPI's for each team member** – any more than this and the team member gets confused – and you get overwhelmed by the amount of data you have to work with.

At the end of each month – arrange a KPI review meeting with each of your team members and go over their performance for the past month – you can also set goals for the next month at the same time.

Make sure you **make your team members aware** of the KPI's you are now tracking and measuring each and every day – as you want them to see how they are performing compared – not only to their individual goals – but to other team members.

Some team members may complain they want to only see their individual results and not the rest of the team – however we find that teams perform better, and are more motivated, when all team members see their results directly compared to their fellow team members.

Let's be honest here – the only team member who does not want their results on display – is the one who is underperforming and not delivering the results you want.

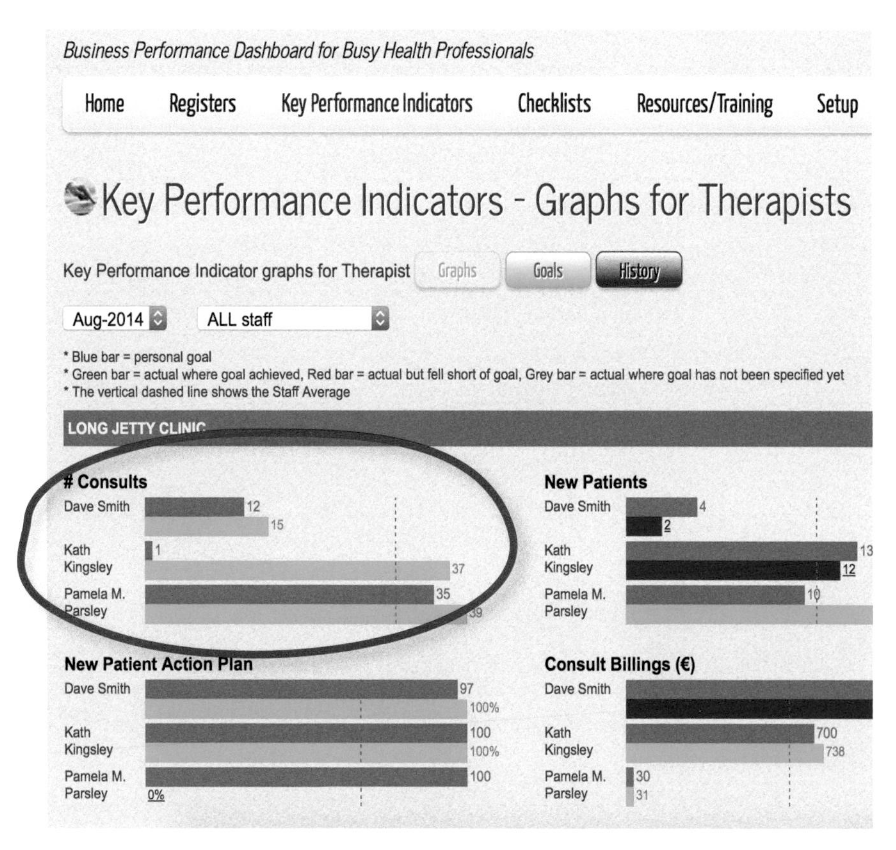

Comparing individual results to the team goal with graphs from inside www.OneMinutePractice.com

Colour coding of **GREEN** (Achieved Goal) and **RED** (Did Not Achieve Goal) greatly increases team motivation and compliance.

"If one of your team members is not performing up to the standards you have set – then your job as a One Minute Practice business owner – is the train this team member to the best of your ability – and if they still do not deliver appropriate performance – let them find a job in another practice – which is more suited to their individual skill set and personality."

Paul Wright

A One Minute Practice fundamental – hire slow and fire fast

Now we move outside the cockpit – to ensuring you always have enough profitable patients filling the passenger cabin of your business via the Marketing Planner.

Secret System Five – Marketing Planner

1. New Patient Register
2. Daily Date Entry
3. Profit and Loss
4. Key Performance Indicators
5. **Marketing Planner**
6. Checklists
7. Ninety Day Goals

The Seven Secret Systems used to run a *One Minute Practice* can be remembered using the first letter from each of the words below:

"New Daily Protocols Keep Money Coming Non-Stop"

The Fifth Secret System – M is for **Marketing Planner**

Secret System Five – the marketing planner

The majority of health businesses lack adequate monitoring – controlling – measuring and assessing their current internal systems and numbers – which is why many owners feel trapped in their clinics – unable to leave for even a few days for fear the systems will fall over and the clinic will fall apart.

For this reason it is always better to focus your marketing efforts on internal systems and processes **BEFORE** you embark on any expensive and time consuming external marketing campaigns.

Earn the right to market your health business

The biggest bang for your buck – as a *One Minute Practice* owner – is to set up and make use of a **good action plan** (or report of findings), **enter and measure your key steps** using your New Patient Register, keep a track of your numbers using the Daily Data Entry, Key Performance Indictor reports and accurately measure your **Profit and Loss** each and every month.

Then and only then have you **really earned the right** – to add new and repeat clients to your business.

If your internal systems are not squeaky clean – you run the risk of pouring water into a leaking bucket.

Assuming you now have your New Patient Register and Daily Data Entry instrumentation feeding good date into the instrumentation in your cockpit (showing your P&L and KPI's), now is the time to make sure your airliner does not run out of passengers!

The Marketing Planner will ensure you maintain a stream of profitable patients coming into your practice.

"The success of a business, particularly in tough times when it's even more important, is closely related to how much time, energy and money its leaders can direct to marketing."

V's

"How much time and energy is consumed dealing with internal problems."

Mal Emery, Author of *Crisis Exposed – Recession Proof Your Business and Income*

Key components of a *One Minute Practice* marketing plan

Type of Event/activity

a) Internal Event – marketing to your database of past clients
b) External Event – marketing to potential new clients

Event/activity title and date – details of the actual event or activity.

Person assigned – who is the team member responsible for creating the material and conducting this specific event or promotion.

Materials required – what resources or material are required for this marketing event – eg brochure, lecture content, webpage.

Status – is the event Pending or Completed?

Results of event – what were the final results for the campaign or event – ie. consults generated, new patients gained, hits to website etc.

Essential components of a sample marketing plan from www.OneMinutePractice.com

Keep a close eye on your current referral sources

One of the best marketing strategies all *One Minute Practice* owners can use is to look closely at the "Referral Source" column in your New Patient Register – and look for any trends or opportunities.

What you are looking for are current referral sources that would be r**elatively easy to increase** – for example – you may notice you are getting referrals from the personal trainers at the local gym – so a great strategy would be to contact the gym manager and arrange a regular in-service or monthly training session for their personal training team.

Add this initiative to your marketing planner – each month keep turning up for the in-service – and reaping the rewards of a consistent and sustained marketing activity.

It is much **easier to increase the number of referrals** you receive from a current referral source – than to generate totally new referrals from somewhere else.

The best businesses have a systematic and highly repetitive marketing system.

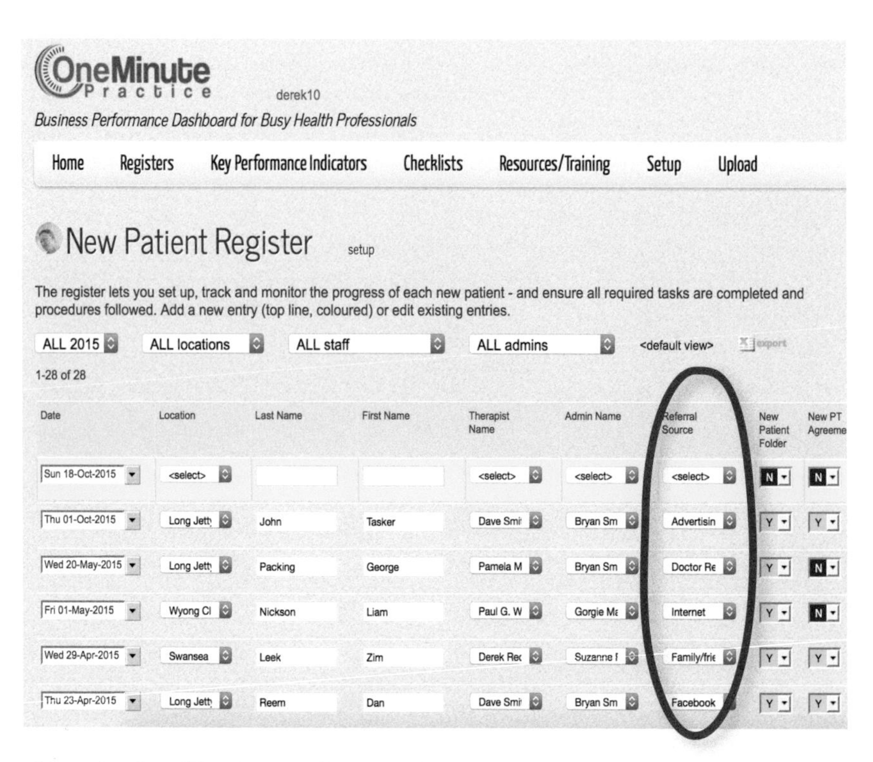

Watch the "Referral Source" column on your New Patient Register for referral source trends – screenshot from www.OneMinutePractice.com

Essential Internal Marketing System – Number One

A one month follow up call list

Of all the marketing strategies available to health business owners – the best and most effective method is a **follow up phone call to your past patient list**.

My favorite ever follow up call system involves exporting a list of patients from your Practice Management Software system who attended your clinic in a certain period of time – but have not had a treatment session since.

For example – if it is now the start of July – export the list of patients who had a consultation in the month of May – but have not had a session since – then call each of these clients.

Each month you should be exporting this list of past patients from your PMS and calling them to make sure all is OK – and if not – making a review consultation.

This simple follow up call system – particularly when combined with the golden question of "**are you now 100%**" – will typically see a rebooking rate of 20% – so 1 in 5 of these past clients will make a review session with you or your team – and there is no marketing system on the planet that can get even close to a 20% success rate.

You can import a list generated by your Practice Management system into the *One Minute Practice* software program which will automatically populate your One Month Follow Up Call register with the client details and make it easy for your staff to record the results of your follow up calls.

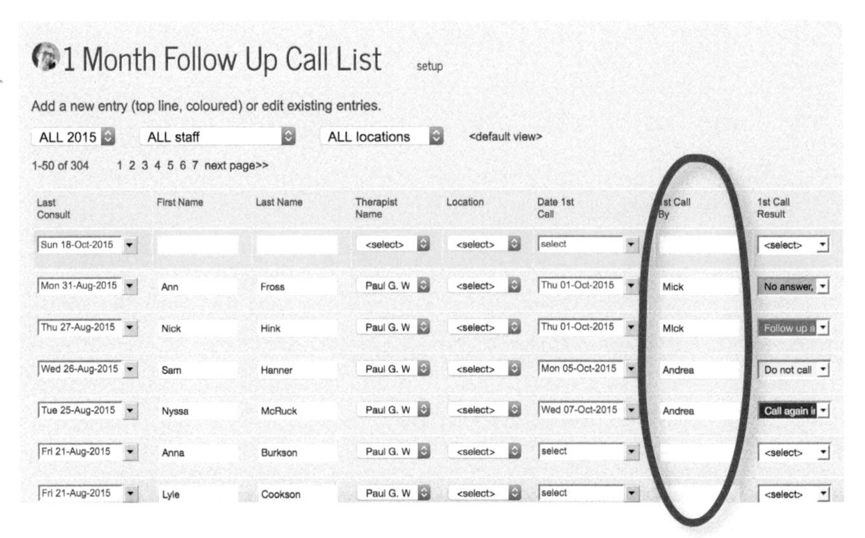

1 Month Follow Up Call List setup

Add a new entry (top line, coloured) or edit existing entries.

ALL 2015 | ALL staff | ALL locations | <default view>

1-50 of 304 1 2 3 4 5 6 7 next page>>

Last Consult	First Name	Last Name	Therapist Name	Location	Date 1st Call	st Call By	1st Call Result
Sun 18-Oct-2015			<select>	<select>	select		<select>
Mon 31-Aug-2015	Ann	Fross	Paul G. W	<select>	Thu 01-Oct-2015	Mick	No answer,
Thu 27-Aug-2015	Nick	Hink	Paul G. W	<select>	Thu 01-Oct-2015	Mick	Follow up a
Wed 26-Aug-2015	Sam	Hanner	Paul G. W	<select>	Mon 05-Oct-2015	Andrea	Do not call
Tue 25-Aug-2015	Nyssa	McRuck	Paul G. W	<select>	Wed 07-Oct-2015	Andrea	Call again i
Fri 21-Aug-2015	Anna	Burkson	Paul G. W	<select>	select		<select>
Fri 21-Aug-2015	Lyle	Cookson	Paul G. W	<select>	select		<select>

A team members name in the "1st call by" column indicates that a call has at least been attempted on a sample one month follow up call list from www.OneMinutePractice.com

Essential Internal Marketing System – Number Two

The cancellation/DNA call list

We have already spoken about the importance of making a phone call to past patients who have fallen out of treatment for some reason – and we are on top of this by using the One Month Follow Up Call List.

However – an equally important list of past clients – are those who have cancelled a recent appointment and not made a follow up consult – or those who have failed to attend a recent scheduled appointment and do not have another session booked.

These Cancellation and DNA clients – are at serious risk of falling through the cracks and not getting a satisfactory outcome unless we take serious steps to contact them and get them back into the clinic to continue their treatment program.

You can import a list generated by your Practice Management system into the *One Minute Practice* software program which will automatically populate your Cancellation/DNA Call register with the client details and make it easy for your staff to record the results of your follow up calls.

You should get an 80% re-booking rate for this marketing system

The re-booking rate for the calls to your Cancellation/DNA Call Register – should be much higher than the 20% re-booking rate we expect for the One Month Call List – because your Cancellation/DNA list are clients who have a fresh injury and have been scheduled for a treatment session already – so we know they are not 100% and still need our help.

The average re-booking rate for these calls to your recently **Cancelled/DNA call list should be over 80%** – especially if your admin team can get these patients entered into the Cancellation/DNA list as soon as possible after their recent cancellation or non attendance.

Your job as a *One Minute Practice* owner is to ensure that your therapists are trained in delivering this call so they are at least getting an 80% re-booking rate – but also checking these calls are actually being made and the result recorded in the Cancellation/ DNA system.

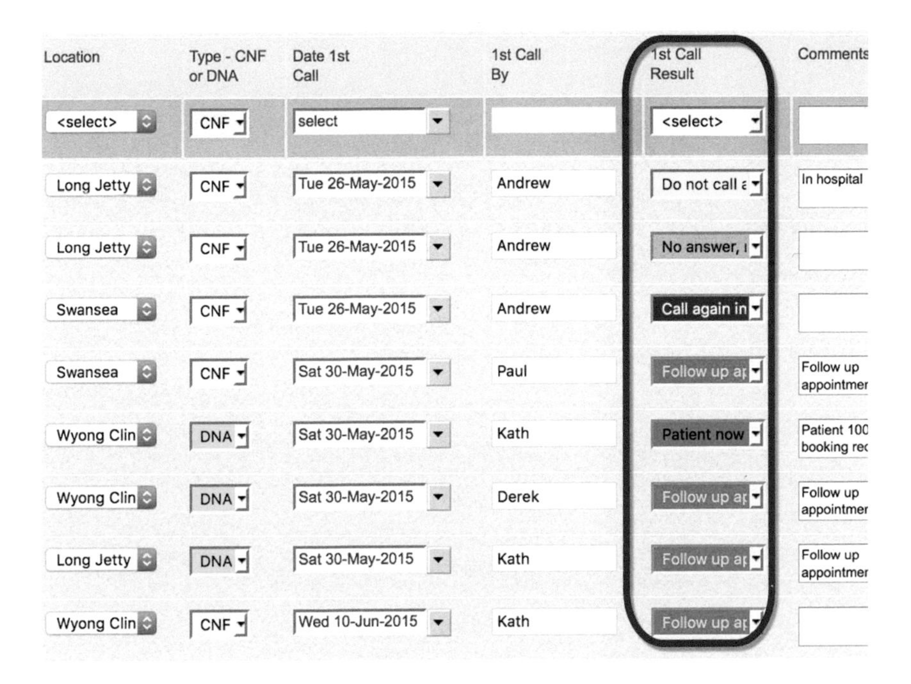

Location	Type - CNF or DNA	Date 1st Call	1st Call By	1st Call Result	Comments
<select>	CNF	select		<select>	
Long Jetty	CNF	Tue 26-May-2015	Andrew	Do not call a	In hospital
Long Jetty	CNF	Tue 26-May-2015	Andrew	No answer, i	
Swansea	CNF	Tue 26-May-2015	Andrew	Call again in	
Swansea	CNF	Sat 30-May-2015	Paul	Follow up ap	Follow up appointmen
Wyong Clin	DNA	Sat 30-May-2015	Kath	Patient now	Patient 100 booking rec
Wyong Clin	DNA	Sat 30-May-2015	Derek	Follow up ap	Follow up appointmen
Long Jetty	DNA	Sat 30-May-2015	Kath	Follow up ap	Follow up appointmen
Wyong Clin	CNF	Wed 10-Jun-2015	Kath	Follow up ap	

Results of a follow up call on this sample cancellation/ DNA register from www.OneMinutePractice.com a **GREEN** colour indicates a re-booking has been made as a result of this call.

Secret System Six – Checklists

1. New Patient Register
2. Daily Date Entry
3. Profit and Loss
4. Key Performance Indicators
5. Marketing Planner
6. **Checklists**
7. Ninety Day Goals

The Seven Secret Systems used to run a *One Minute Practice* can be remembered using the first letter from each of the words below:

"New Daily Protocols Keep Money Coming Non-Stop"

The Sixth Secret System – C is for Checklists

Secret System Six – checklists

Airlines and Operating Theatres require a high level of certainty, so airline pilots and surgical staff make extensive use of checklists in order to be confident that essential steps have been completed.

Your business is no different.

As we have already seen – the key to owning and operating a *One Minute Practice* and having a life of freedom and success – is to achieve a high level of **certainty** in your business.

You need certainty that each new patient completes the steps and processes in their new client journey – which you measure and track with a comprehensive **New Patient Register**.

You need certainty that your team are performing to the standards you expect – which you can now measure and track using your **Key Performance Indicators**.

You need certainty that your business is profitable by staying on top of the **Profit and Loss**.

However – you also need to be certain the many regular and routine tasks you expect all therapists, administration team members and even **you the owner** need to complete – are actually being done in your business.

We have lost count of the number of times we have seen a business owner set or allocate a team member a new task – only to revisit that task a week or two later – and find that the task has not been completed and the team member has forgotten all about it.

That's why you need a **checklist system** in your *One Minute Practice.*

A fundamental checklist mistake

Do not make the mistake of just telling your team about their respective checklist items – and expecting the team members to pick up the ball and run with it – this is a recipe for *One Minute Practice* failure.

Successful *One Minute Practice* owners – call a general team meeting and give an overview of the individual checklists they have set up for the admin, therapists and for themselves – and at this team meeting everyone is made aware that daily checklist completion is **not negotiable**.

The owner then keeps a close eye on the team's checklists – and the first time they see a team member fail to complete it – they are quickly in contact with the offending team member and the error is corrected.

The secret to owning a One Minute Practice – is again – being able to quickly and easily assess the key steps are being followed, the team are all on track, and all tasks are being completed.

Once the checklist is up and running – you can allocate your clinic or admin manager to oversee that all checklists are being completed each day, week, month and year.

The *One Minute Practice* software makes this very easy to do – as you can see from the screenshot on the following pages of administration team members and therapists checklists.

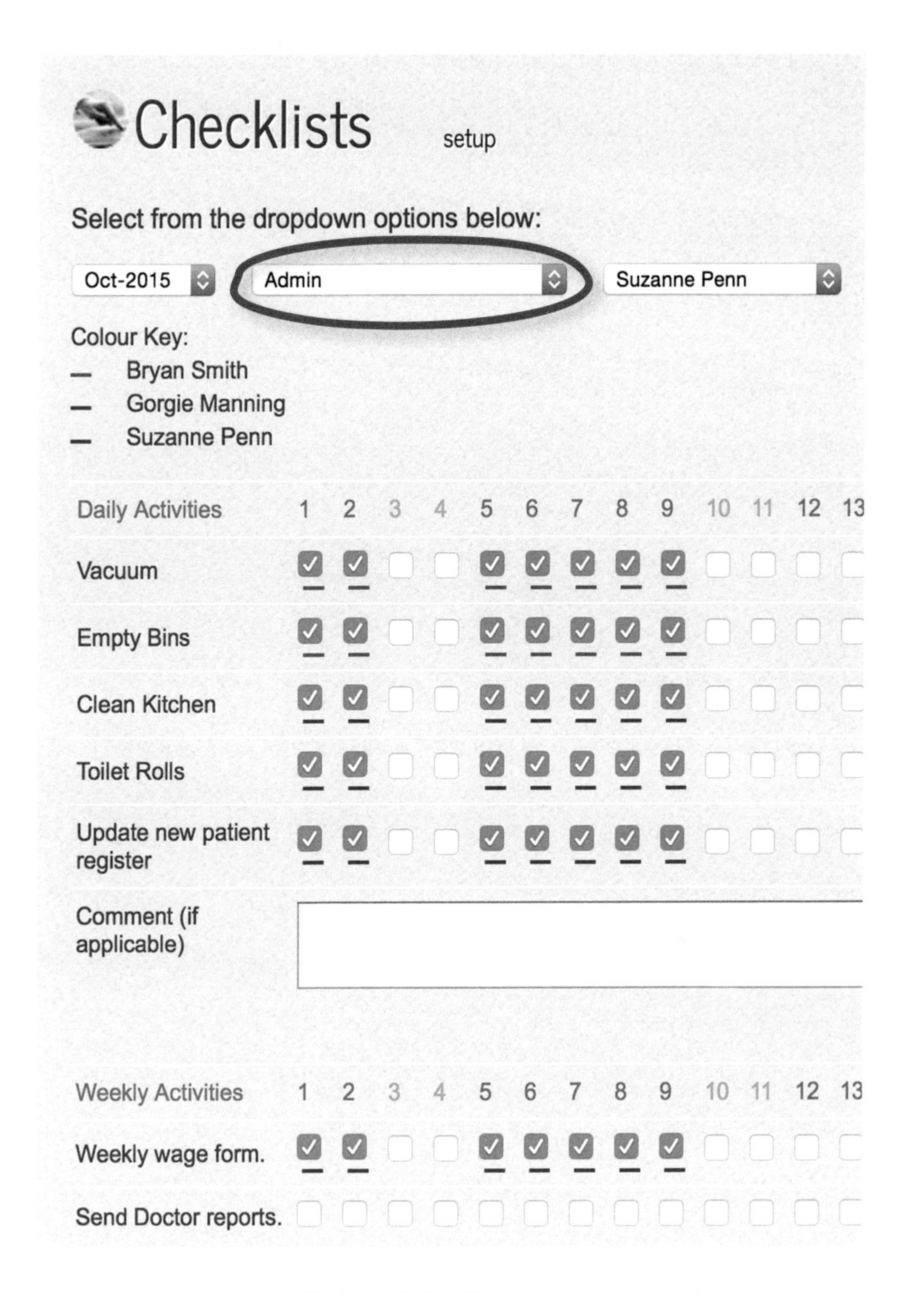

An example of an Administration team member checklist from www.OneMinutePractice.com

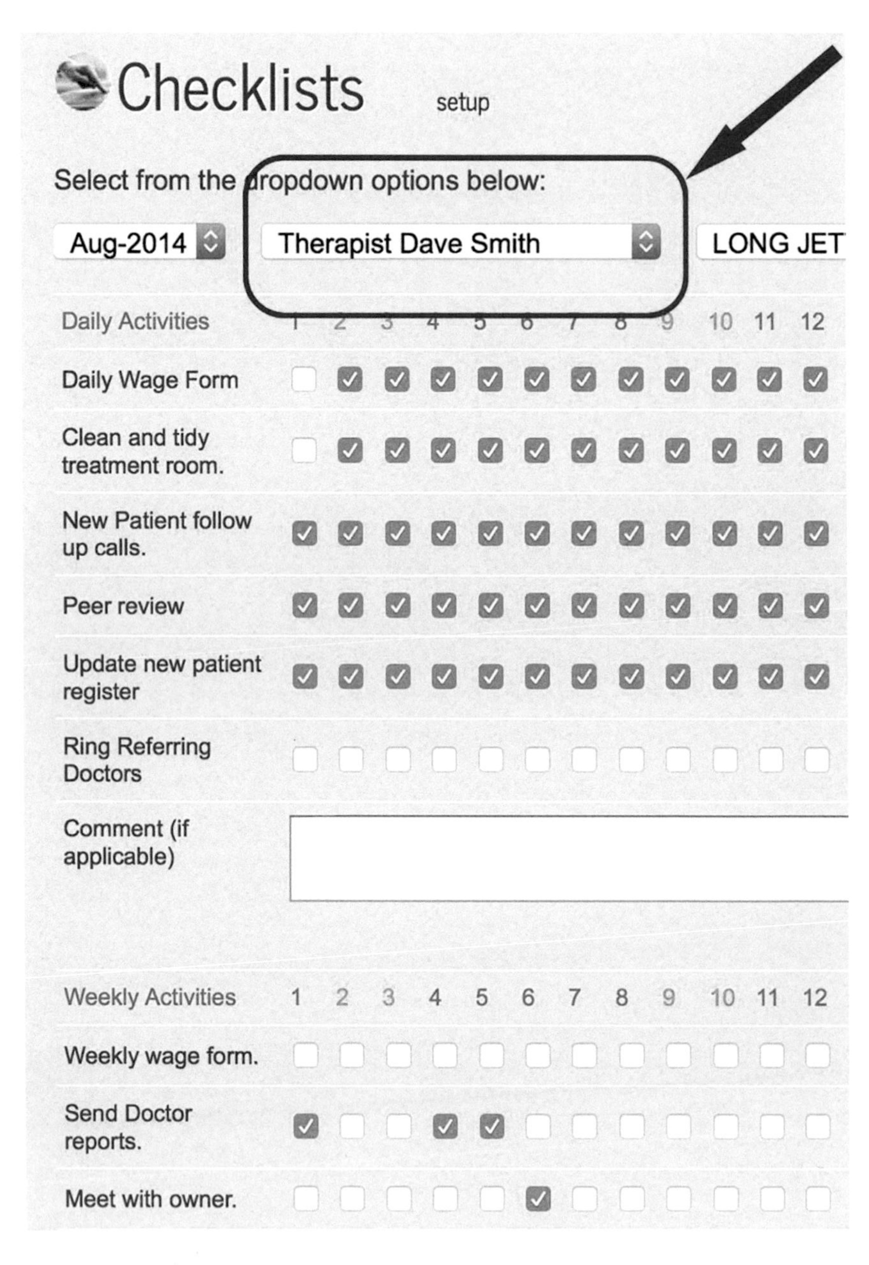

An Example of Therapists Team Checklist from www.OneMinutePractice.com

Secret System Seven – Ninety Day Goals

1. New Patient Register
2. Daily Date Entry
3. Profit and Loss
4. Key Performance Indicators
5. Marketing Planner
6. Checklists
7. **Ninety Day Goals**

The Seven Secret Systems used to run a *One Minute Practice* can be remembered using the first letter from each of the words below:

"New Daily Protocols Keep Money Coming Non-Stop"

The Seventh Secret System – N is for **Ninety Day Goals**

Secret System Seven – Ninety Day Goals

One of the most important parts of running a *One Minute Practice* program is a the inclusion of a comprehensive Ninety Day Goal section – where you and your team are able to set and monitor – not only individual goals – but the completion and progress of the action steps that need to be taken to complete these goals.

All successful *One Minute Practice* owners must have a monthly review meeting with each team members where they collectively review not only their KPI's (which we have already covered in the KPI section) – but the setting, monitoring and achieving of the team members Ninety Day Goals.

These monthly sessions allow you to refocus your team and help them get what they want from their time as part of your organisation.

Then at the end of the Ninety day goal period – your monthly meeting is then focusing on evaluating the achievement of these goals – and then setting the new Ninety days goals for the next quarter.

The Ninety Day Goals MUST include definite action steps not just a list of goals

At *One Minute Practice* we believe setting the Ninety Day Goal is only part of the battle – we then want you to describe the exact action steps you and your team need to take over the next ninety days to achieve each goal.

For example – to achieve my Ninety Day Goal of "**Hiring a New Therapist**" I will need to do take the following action steps:

- Place employment notices in association magazine
- Arrange interviews with the five top applicants
- Finalise contracts with new team member
- Complete the therapist induction

Once you have added the action steps for each goal – you can then add a comment to each action step and add the date that step has been completed.

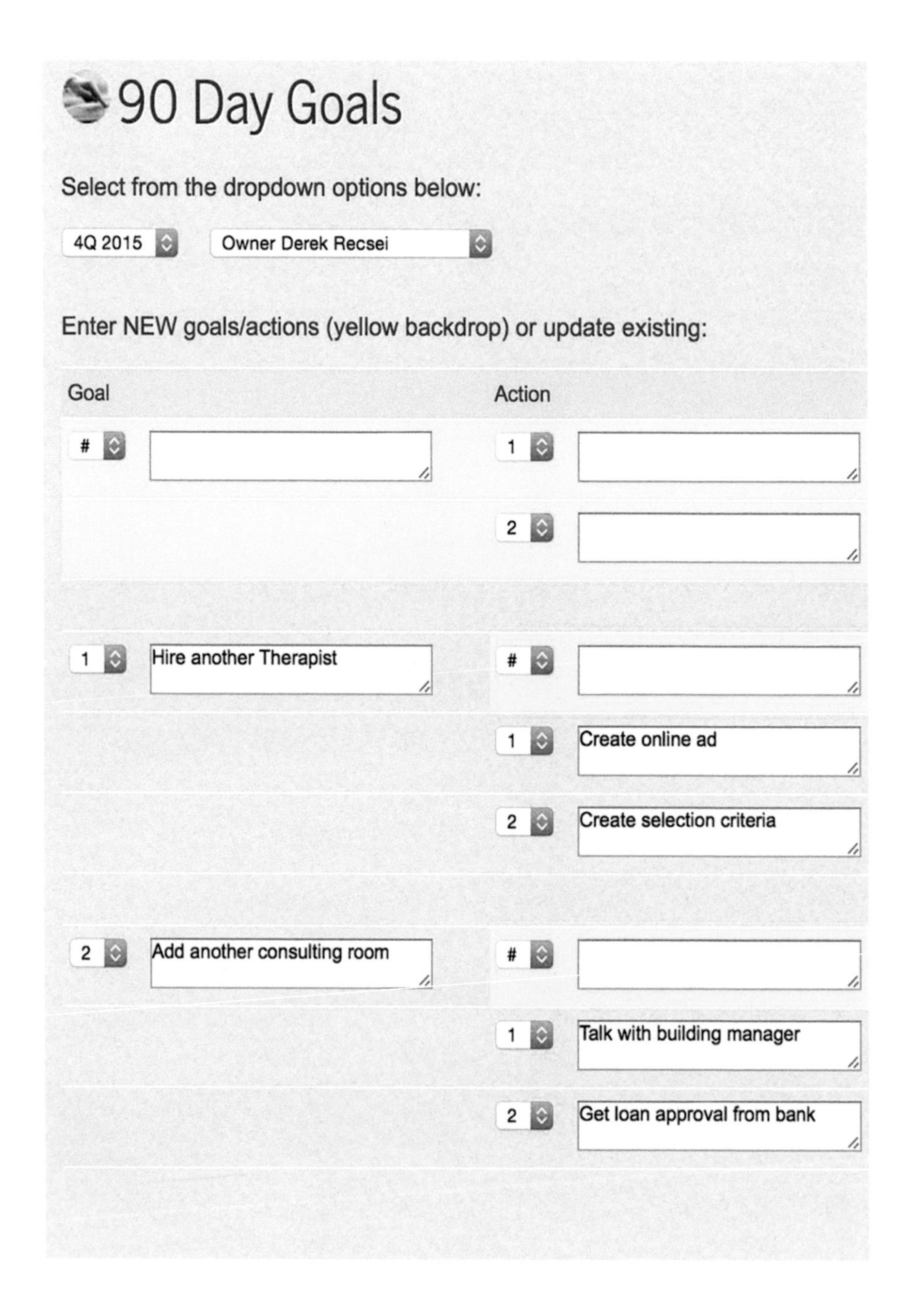

90 Day Goals
Select from the dropdown options below:
4Q 2015
Owner Derek Recsei
Enter NEW goals/actions (yellow backdrop) or update existing:
Goal
Action
#
1
2
1
Hire another Therapist
#
1
Create online ad
2
Create selection criteria
2
Add another consulting room
#
1
Talk with building manager
2
Get loan approval from bank

You must have a goal and a list of Action Steps to achieve this goal in your Ninety Day Goal System – here is a sample Ninety Day Goals screenshot from www.OneMinutePractice.com

Get started on your Ninety Day Goals NOW

The inclusion of a structured and strategic Ninety Day Goals program is an incredibly powerful and important part of running a *One Minute Practice*.

We can guarantee that if you diligently set up and monitor your Ninety days goals and the completion of the related action steps – you will be amazed at the increased productivity you and your team will see.

The Seven Secret Systems – Summary

To run a true One Minute Practice – you need to systematically and strategically implement the "Seven Secret Systems" we have covered in this book.

1. **New Patient Register** – record and measure the critical success steps in your health business.
2. **Daily Date Entry** – collect the key numbers used to measure your team and business performance.
3. **Profit and Loss** – know not only if your business is profitable but where you need to tighten up and where money may be leaking from your current business.
4. **Key Performance Indicators (KPI's)** – measure, motivate and challenge your team to be the best they can be.
5. **Marketing Planner** – oversee and control the key components that keep new and current clients coming back to see you.
6. **Checklists** – instantly know that all key tasks are being completed across your business.
7. **Ninety Day Goals** – build team morale, increase productivity and ensure all team members are getting exactly what they want from their time in your organisation.

The final chapter – how to be a true *One Minute Practice* owner

The *One Minute Practice* program has the power to totally transform your health business – just like it has done for health business owners around the world in many different professions.

That being said – do not get overwhelmed and think you need to be doing all of the Seven Secret Systems straight away.

Even worse – DO NOT procrastinate by putting your head in the sand and DO NOTHING.

The smartest *One Minute Practice* owners – start slowly – gradually adding the next Secret System **ONLY** when their team are confident and effectively using the parts of the program they have already launched.

An easy introduction to a *One Minute Practice*

Begin your *One Minute Practice* journey with a basic action plan or report of findings – and track your key protocols by using a simple **New Patient Register**.

Start collecting basic data using your **Daily Data Entry** platform.

Over the next month or two – using the data from the New Patient Register and the Daily Data Entry you will decide on the best and most effective **Key Performance Indicators** so you can start setting team goals and comparing one therapist to the next.

Then it is time to get on top of your **Profit and Loss** – so you know if your business is following industry trends and where you may need to make some changes.

Next step is to meet with your team and develop your **Ninety Days Goals and Action Steps** – to get you and your team moving in the right direction.

Then add and start monitoring your team **Checklists** – so you are certain all tasks are being completed – even when you are not there.

Finally move into the exciting world of the **Marketing Planner** and add your two big gun internal marketing steps – the **One Month Follow Up Call List** and the **Cancellation/DNA Call Register**.

Enjoy the *One Minute Practice* lifestyle

As a smart One Minute Practice health business owner – once the majority of the systems are set up – you quickly review your New Patient Register, scan the Key Performance Indicators, check the Profit and Loss, run your eye over the Checklists , make sure the Follow Up and Cancellation/DNA Calls are being made – and the key activities on the Marketing Planner are being looked after.

Then get on with whatever you want to be doing – **like spending time with your family** or pursuing your favourite hobby.

This daily review of the systems should take you no more than **ONE MINUTE**.

1 min

One Minute Practice mistake number one

Launching a program or protocol (eg. a New Patient Register or Checklist) and not fully monitoring that it is being completed and used by your team each and every day.

1

2

One Minute Practice mistake number two

Moving onto the next One Minute Practice Secret System when the current procedure is not being completed and performed correctly each and every time.

One Minute Practice mistake number three

Giving in to your team when they complain about adding a new protocol or procedure.

Most team members prefer things to stay just the way they are – even if you are doing all the work and making no money.

It is **YOUR business** – you decide how things are done.

One Minute Practice mistake number four

Failing to delegate a large amount of the One Minute Practice setup work to your team members.

There is no doubt each of the Seven Secret Systems – can take some time and effort to setup – however make sure you delegate whatever steps you can in this process.

Get your admin team to create their own checklists and ask your therapists to create their own action plans and Ninety Day Goals.

5

One Minute Practice mistake number five

Failing to have consequences for lack of task completion or poor performance.

Never accept poor compliance or performance as "Just the way it is" or shrug your shoulders and say "What can you do?".

This attitude will chain you to your business forever – never accept things as "Just the Way They Are".

One Minute Practice mistake number six

Failing to have the difficult conversations

"Success in business and in life – is largely determined by the number of difficult conversations you are willing to have". Unknown

If a team member has been trained well and still does not complete set protocols or perform at the standard required you have an obligation to yourself, your current team and the offending team member – to let them find a position more suited to their specific skill set.

Remember – "Hire Slow and Fire Fast".

6

Final Words

As we approach the end of our *One Minute Practice* journey you are left with one of two choices.

You can keep running your health business the way you have always done it – with heavy reliance on you, enjoying little or no freedom, and feeling totally overwhelmed by the amount of work you have to do each and every day.

OR

You can join the elite band of health business owners who have taken control of their business and their lives by using the "Seven Secret Systems" of the One Minute Practice program.

The choice is yours.

Free Bonuses. Bonus resources for all readers

Make sure you go to the website below to access a range of great bonus resources that will help you run a *One Minute Practice.*

At this page you can download a sample Action Plan, a New Patient Agreement, a Welcome Email, a New Patient Letter and a New Patient Feedback form you can copy and use in your health business immediately.

www.OneMinutePracticeBookBonus.com

You can also register to watch a FREE video that takes you inside the *One Minute Practice* online health business tracking program upon which this book is based.

Good luck in your *One Minute Practice*

If you have any questions you need help with go to the "contact us" tab on the home page at **www.oneminutepractice.com** – email **admin@healthbusinessprofits.com** or submit a support ticket to **www.healthbusinessprofits.com/msupport**

If you want to learn more about internal systems, marketing your health business or how to increase the productivity of your front desk team – make sure you register for and watch my free webinars – which you can find at the **www.healthbusinessprofits.com** home page – and also in the resources section of the *One Minute Practice* Program.

We wish you well in your health business journey and can't wait to hear how One Minute Practice has transformed your business and your life.

Good Luck

Paul Wright

Would you like Paul Wright to speak at your next allied health conference or event?

Paul is available as a speaker and consultant to allied health professionals and associations on the subject of Health Business Management, Marketing and Passive Income Creation.

Paul can be contacted at:

E: admin@healthbusinessprofits.com

P: (02) 4971 6988 – Australia

W: www.OneMinutePractice.com
www.HealthBusinessProfits.com
www.PhysioProfessor.com

M: Physio Professor Pty Ltd.
PO Box 574,
Swansea, NSW, Australia, 2281

What seminar attendees have said about Paul Wright presentations:

"Spectacular – I Loved It – Within the First Hour I Learnt Enough to Make Me an Extra $20,000" Lise, Physiotherapist

"Why didn't I find this guy 15 years ago – I now know how to put everything into my practice to make my health business hum, quit working quite so hard in my business so I can work more on my business and start to realise the profits" Cherye – Chiropractor

"Excellent – Paul's willingness to give of his experience and draw on years of practical and real world tangible stuff was fantastic. Highly recommended – if you don't do this course you are nuts." Ted – Podiatrist.

"Three years ago I came across one of Paul's videos and I have since gone from a single practitioner business to having a thriving business with eleven professionals." Albert – Physiotherapist

"Every country in the world has to have Paul up for a conference – the talk he did today was exceptional" Darryl – Physiotherapist

"Excellent delivery. Valuable information gained. Very impressed" Dave, Massage Therapist

"This should be a part of the University Health Professional course" Ian, Physiotherapist

About Paul Wright

Since graduating as a Physical Education teacher in 1987 and as a physiotherapist in 1990 Paul Wright has opened many multi-disciplinary health clinics, closed a few, been locked out of one and sold some others – over this time he has employed countless therapists and support staff.

Paul has been actively involved in clinical education around the world having lectured to thousands of health professionals in the areas of program design, injury prevention, rehabilitation and business development and even found the time to win multiple titles as a competitive bodybuilder.

Paul Wright is living proof the" Ultimate Health Business Lifestyle" is possible.

At one stage he owned six successful Get Active Physiotherapy clinics in Australia, yet still spent more time at home than his wife preferred, never missed a school concert or sports carnival, and visited his clinics for only a few hours each week. While doing this he did not even live in the same city as 5 of his clinics!

Since selling his health businesses Paul now prefers spending even more time with his family and friends, at the beach, or at home working on the Million Dollar Health Professional Program, Profit Club, One on One Coaching, The Practice Acceleration Program, The Ultimate Patient Attraction System, The Ultimate Front Desk Training System, presenting live seminars and working on his PhysioProfessor.com and thePTProfessor.com online education portals.

His latest passion is the "One Minute Practice" online health business tracking and monitoring program – upon which this book is based – you can find out more about this incredible program at:

www.OneMinutePractice.com

For Even More Paul Wright Resources and FREE Webinars – go to:

www.HealthBusinessProfits.com